CRITIC

CRITICAL THINKING

JONATHAN HABER

The MIT Press | Cambridge, Massachusetts | London, England

This book was set in Chaparral Pro by Toppan Best-set Premedia Limited. Printed and bound in the United States of America.

Library of Congress Cataloging-in-Publication Data is available.

ISBN: 978-0-262-53828-2

10   9   8   7   6   5   4   3   2   1A

To Mom and Dad
for teaching me to think

CONTENTS

SERIES FOREWORD

The MIT Press Essential Knowledge series offers accessible, concise, beautifully produced pocket-size books on topics of current interest. Written by leading thinkers, the books in this series deliver expert overviews of subjects that range from the cultural and the historical to the scientific and the technical.

In today's era of instant information gratification, we have ready access to opinions, rationalizations, and superficial descriptions. Much harder to come by is the foundational knowledge that informs a principled understanding of the world. Essential Knowledge books fill that need. Synthesizing specialized subject matter for nonspecialists and engaging critical topics through fundamentals, each of these compact volumes offers readers a point of access to complex ideas.

Bruce Tidor
Professor of Biological Engineering and Computer Science
Massachusetts Institute of Technology

In a 2009 address focusing on national education policy, President Barack Obama issued this challenge:

> I'm calling on our nation's governors and state education chiefs to develop standards and assessments that don't simply measure whether students can fill in a bubble on a test, but whether they possess 21st century skills like problem-solving and critical thinking and entrepreneurship and creativity.[1]

A manifestation of this national priority was the Common Core, a set of language and math standards initially implemented in forty-six US states, standards that prioritize "developing the critical-thinking, problem-solving, and analytical skills students will need to be successful."[2]

Two decades earlier, President George H. W. Bush announced his administration's "America 2000" educational initiative, which expressed the following objective as part of "Goal 5: Adult Literacy and Lifelong Learning": that "The proportion of college graduates who demonstrate advanced ability to think critically, communicate effectively, and solve problems will increase substantially."[3]

These national education priorities, and other initiatives and research projects that stretch back more than a century, stress the importance of *critical thinking*, a type of thinking with characteristics distinct from general intelligence or intellectual virtues such as thoughtfulness and wisdom.

Today, educators and educational reformers across the globe regularly announce that rote learning must give way to the nurturing of critical thinkers, the very type of people in highest demand by employers.

This was illustrated in a 2013 research report by the Association of American College and Universities, which indicated that "More than 75 percent of [employers] surveyed say they want more emphasis on five key areas including: critical thinking, complex problem solving, written and oral communication, and applied knowledge in real-world settings."[4]

In 2018, the Organization for Economic Co-operation and Development (OECD), an international economic development body made up of the world's most economically advanced nations, began a project to study how critical thinking can be taught and assessed in support of "a growing consensus that formal education should cultivate the creativity and critical-thinking skills of students to help them succeed in modern, globalised economies based on knowledge and innovation."[5]

Global economic changes favoring individual innovation over mass production have also triggered interest in developing critical thinkers in countries like China, where a small but growing number of critical-thinking programs in higher education challenge a traditional education system focused on the authority of the teacher passing down established texts. As one researcher observed, "In academic journals and media, the term critical thinking is sometimes used to connote an exit strategy needed to depart from China's age-old education tradition of rote learning."[6]

Beyond economics, our political debates about "fake news" and other hot-button topics imply the importance of reasoning skills that allow us to find truth and make informed decisions. One fallout from the 2016 US presidential election was a sense of crisis regarding voters' ability to make choices through reason rather than through the emotional judgments and/or tribalism that characterize so much of US and world politics today.

As these examples show, in today's world "critical thinking" has taken on a prominent role in global educational debates and the goal of creating critical thinkers now informs major initiatives such as the development of nation-spanning academic standards. One might even assert that acquiring and applying this skill is vital to our survival as a society, if not a species. That said, I wonder how many people, if asked, could answer this question: What is critical thinking?

My own attempt to answer the question has been informed by a range of experiences, including work with employers on techniques to assess and measure critical-thinking and other cognitive skills, as well as building critical-thinking principles into curricula and assessments related to a digital-literacy education. Over time, my interest in applying critical-thinking principles more broadly led to development of *Critical Voter*,[7] a curriculum and set of related teacher resources that used the 2012 presidential election to teach many of the critical thinking skills described in this book such as logic, argumentation, language skills (including persuasive communication), and controlling for biases.

Before releasing *Critical Voter* to wider audiences, its precepts were tested through "prototype" lessons taught to my own children, one of whom will have started college by the time this manuscript is completed.

My son being in college might not necessarily be good news critical-thinking wise. According to Richard Alum and Josipa Roska in their popular 2011 book *Academically Adrift*, "gains in critical thinking, complex reasoning, and writing skills (i.e., general collegiate skills) during the first two years of college are either exceedingly small or empirically nonexistent for a large proportion of students."[8] This despite the fact that, per a report cited by the authors, "99 percent of college faculty say that developing students' ability to think critically is a 'very important' or 'essential' goal of undergraduate education."[9]

The impact of *Academically Adrift* on discussions and debates about higher education, in both the academic and popular press, demonstrated general acceptance that a world without critical-thinking skills is a world to be feared. But why might this be so?

Built into the conversation about critical thinking taking place in the academy and among the wider public is an assumption that knowledge alone cannot help us solve the problems we face as individuals and as a society.

In the last few decades we have seen rapid acceleration in the creation of new knowledge coupled with unparalleled access to information through digital devices that are our constant companions. Yet errors in judgment continue to plague us at the individual and societal levels.

Worse, our inability to evaluate the information contained in our myriad pocket "Libraries of Alexandria" in terms of its veracity and credibility means we are just as likely to believe false information and draw incorrect conclusions from such "facts," some of them fed to us by those who understand the flaws in human reasoning well enough to manipulate us.

Some commentary on the 2016 US election concluded that many Americans make decisions based on emotion rather than reason, implying that the public's ability to think critically does not exist or is easily short-circuited. But one need not look to national politics to see problems associated with lack of critical thinking. How many impulsive purchases, bad career choices, needless arguments with loved ones, and other personal problems might be

Errors in judgment
continue to plague
us at the individual
and societal levels.

avoided if we could train our minds to locate and evaluate evidence, place it into a structure for analysis, and base our choices on rules that have informed sound judgment since the days of Socrates and Aristotle?

Since controlling for bias is an important critical-thinking skill, one discussed throughout this book, I should share up front a conviction that has fueled my years of work in this field: that the most important critical-thinking issue facing the world today is that not enough people are doing enough of it, which explains this book's emphasis on how critical thinking can be taught, practiced and evaluated.

Teaching ourselves and others to become critical thinkers requires a grounding in core principles, so to guide readers through what this book covers:

Chapter 1, "The Genealogy of Critical Thinking," explains the origins of the term in the context of the disciplines critical thinking draws upon, such as philosophy, psychology, and science. This chapter introduces early definitions for "critical thinking," definitional issues being a subject that comes up frequently in discussions of the topic. My contribution to that discussion is not to lobby for my own preferred definition, but to instead help readers better understand the concept by introducing them to critical thinking's fascinating origins.

Chapter 2, "Components of Critical Thinking" looks at the knowledge, skills, and personal dispositions required to be a critical thinker. Despite widely varying content choices and practices by critical-thinking educators, this chapter proposes that there is a consensus regarding what critical thinkers should know and be able to do.

Chapter 3, "Defining, Teaching, and Assessing Critical Thinking," begins with a deeper discussion of how researchers define "critical thinking" as well as how the concept might fit into broader frameworks. I contend that this work has generated sufficient insight to move forward with the vital project of increasing the amount of critical thinking in the world. How this can be done is covered in the remainder of this chapter, which describes research and practice regarding how critical thinking can be taught and assessed.

While educators are the target audience for this book, my vision of who falls into that category is expansive, including instructors at postsecondary institutions fortunate enough to teach the subject full-time, as well as K–12 teachers trying to instill critical-thinking abilities in students learning math, science, reading, writing, history, and any other discipline requiring higher-order thinking. It also includes parents who want to raise children to think for themselves. Finally, it includes everyone on any kind of educational journey, in the classroom or on their own, who longs to think more effectively and live in a world where decisions are made through reason and thoughtful deliberation.

THE GENEALOGY OF
CRITICAL THINKING

Where did the idea originate that there is a form of thinking unique enough to be termed "critical?"

As the creation of critical thinkers became an educational priority, teachers, policy makers, and researchers tried to understand critical thinking in ways comparable to existing academic disciplines. The learning process for skills such as reading and writing or disciplines such as mathematics, chemistry, and biology involves a step-by-step acquisition of abilities and an understanding of the body of knowledge that constitutes each subject. Anyone studying chemistry, for example, learns how that discipline is defined (usually along the lines of dictionary definitions such as "a science that deals with the composition, structure, and properties of substances and with the transformations that they undergo"[1]). They also learn about atoms and molecules before moving on to the chemical reactions that break and form bonds between atoms in molecules.

Starting in this chapter, you will be introduced to a number of attempts to determine what it means to be a critical thinker, with chapter 2 dedicated to describing various elements that go into the critical-thinking construct and chapter 3 focused on how those elements might fit together in the context of how critical thinking can be defined, taught, and assessed.

One of the skills researchers and educators agree critical thinkers should possess and practice is the ability to look at a problem from different perspectives, which is why this chapter takes a historic/genealogical approach by looking at where and how the idea of critical thinking originated and how it has developed since then.

It all starts with philosophy.

Philosophy

An intellectual explosion that took place from the sixth through the fourth centuries B.C.E. defined many aspects of the world we now take for granted. During this period, for instance, Confucius developed theories of proper human behavior and social organization, which today would be called ethical and political philosophy. In the same era, the practitioners of the Indian Vaisheshika tradition explored metaphysical questions regarding the nature of reality.

In the West, a similar intellectual ferment was occurring in ancient Greece, a land dominated by small city states such as Athens, where Western philosophy was born.

Three figures dominate the origin story of Greek philosophy. The first, Socrates, questioned fixed beliefs and strove to live an "examined life," activities that earned him the title of father of Western philosophy as well as a death sentence from his annoyed fellow Athenians. Socrates left behind no written work, but others captured his insights, notably his student Plato, whose *Dialogs* presents his master's thinking intertwined with his own ideas. Plato also founded what is considered to be the first school of philosophy in the Western world—the Academy—where philosophers such as the brilliant Aristotle studied.

The ideas of these ancient thinkers undergirds much of Western thought, summed up in a quote by the famous twentieth-century philosopher and mathematician Alfred North Whitehead, who described the entire Western philosophical tradition as a "series of footnotes to Plato."[2] To understand the origins of critical thinking, however, we need to look at the key works of Plato's student Aristotle.

To grasp Aristotle and classical philosophy generally, keep in mind that today's distinction between philosophy and science did not exist in the ancient world. The work of

To understand the
origins of critical
thinking, however,
we need to look at the
key works of Plato's
student Aristotle.

the earliest Greek philosophers (called the pre-Socratics), for example, focused on the nature of the physical world. While their ideas—such as the world being made of water or fire or magnets as living beings—seem naive today, these thinkers acted as early physicists formulating physical, rather than magical or religious, explanations for natural phenomena.

One of the roles Aristotle played was that of a great systematizer who brought order to a wide range of subjects studied by him and other thinkers. In fact, many of today's academic fields, such as biology and political science, became distinct disciplines only when Aristotle analyzed and organized them.

His approach, unique at the time, was to gather evidence and examples that he used to create systems that defined a field. For instance, Aristotle's study of plants and animals (some specimens provided from conquered lands by his student Alexander the Great) led to a classification system based on physical characteristics, a forerunner to the biology taxonomy used today to categorize living things. Likewise, in his book *Politics*, Aristotle classified the constitutions of contemporaneous political entities as "specimens" of political organization and then synthesized his classification system into a structure that defined the field of political science.

Aristotle also wrote original works on logic that introduced systems for classifying information, methods for organizing and analyzing logical arguments, types of reasoning errors (fallacies), and many other concepts discussed in the next chapter's exploration of structured thinking. Similarly, his work on language, called *Rhetoric*, underlies how the words and phrases used to present ideas and arguments can be selected and structured to persuade. The role language plays in critical thinking is also discussed in chapter 2.

Many of Aristotle's works were lost for centuries. They have been rediscovered, however, at different times and subsequently used alongside other classical texts to help launch new eras of intellectual exploration. But even when his specific words were not being read, the ideas he generated—especially those regarding logic and rhetoric—became the building blocks of education for centuries.

The schooling of ancient Greeks and Romans, for example, began with the so-called *trivium*, which involved studying logic, rhetoric, and grammar (language and composition). Once those subjects were mastered, students moved on to the *quadrivium* of arithmetic, geometry, astronomy, and music. These subjects and those of the trivium established the seven liberal arts of the ancient world. While not always framed within the trivium/quadrivium framework, subjects such as logic and rhetoric continued to define what it meant to be an educated person throughout the Middle Ages and well into the modern era.

When I was in college in the 1980s, one professor offered a course titled "The Quadrivium" that served as a modern approach to teaching the latter set of liberal arts subjects. While similar experimentation has occurred at various liberal arts schools, interest in trivium-style learning is most pronounced today in some segments of the American home-schooling movement, where classical and religious education mix freely. These small nods to the elements of ancient thought, along with the role logic plays in every discussion of critical thinking, demonstrate the ongoing pull of a "love of wisdom"—the definition of philosophy—on those seeking to instill more than just knowledge in learners.

The Renaissance, Scientific Revolution, and Age of Enlightenment

Another series of intellectual and political upheavals that played out in Europe starting in the fourteenth century led to more revolutions in thinking that contributed key elements to what would come to be considered critical thinking.

The European Renaissance of the fourteenth through seventeenth centuries is remembered as a flourishing period of art, architecture, and engineering. During that era, "Renaissance men" like Michelangelo and Leonardo Da

Vinci created not just artistic masterpieces but great engineering breakthroughs such as urban fortifications and early designs for flying machines. "Renaissance" means "rebirth," and one of the primary drivers for this resurgence of intellectual independence was the rediscovery of classic works of Greek and Roman philosophy unearthed from European monasteries or smuggled into the West from a crumbling Byzantine Empire.[3]

The term "Scientific Revolution" refers to a period that started in the fifteenth century when breakthroughs in mathematics and the physical sciences, discovered through new approaches to inquiry, led to great and controversial discoveries like the earth not being at the center of the universe.

The popular shorthand version of this history describes how Europe's "Dark Ages," during which the Catholic church held sway over men's minds, ended when gallant scientists like Copernicus and Galileo insisted—and demonstrated through mathematical calculation and scientific observation—that the earth orbited the sun rather than vice versa. The success of this type of scientific thinking inspired others to slough off religious dogma and think for themselves in rational, scientific ways.

As usual, real history is not so simple. For instance, the church dogma early scientists fought against had as much to do with ancient Greek philosophy and science as it did with biblical texts. The idea of God as infinitely

The success of this type of scientific thinking inspired others to slough off religious dogma and think for themselves in rational, scientific ways.

powerful, knowledgeable, and good, or heaven as a place of perfection separate from our physical realm, has very little support in the Hebrew Bible or New Testament. But ideas of such perfect "forms" flourished in Greek philosophy, especially the works of Plato.[4] When the Roman Empire converted to Christianity in the fourth century ADE, existing Roman belief systems—many of them built on principles of Greek philosophy—entered Christianity's intellectual bloodstream. Similarly, ancient science found a home in church thinking in the thirteenth century when Thomas Aquinas integrated newly rediscovered works of Aristotle with Christian theology, providing a philosophical and scientific basis for what would become acceptable church beliefs about how the world worked.

Unfortunately, Aristotle's hard science and the vision of nature it represented did not have the staying power of his works on logic. During his own time, Aristotle's method of inferring truths from what the human senses could perceive, rather than explaining natural phenomena as the work of gods, was a tremendous intellectual breakthrough. To pick an example where this approach can fail, however, our sensory experience tells us we are stationary while the sun, moon, and stars move around us. This made the geocentric (earth-centered) system developed by Ptolemy in the second century C.E. intuitive to sense perception and thus valid according to the science of his day through the fifteenth century C.E.

Ptolemy's geocentrism did not explain all observed phenomenon, however. The quirky pathways of the planets through the night skies, for example, did not fit this world view. Such discrepancies inspired scientists like Kepler, Copernicus, and Galileo to propose an alternative heliocentric (sun-centered) theory that better fit with all observations and data. In doing so, however, the dogma they were taking on was as much Aristotelian and Ptolemaic as biblical. Seen in this light, the scientific revolution can be thought of as not shaking off of superstition but replacing one scientific paradigm with another, something we saw last century as Einstein's theory of relativity and the science of quantum mechanics overturned Newton's mechanical view of the universe, or at least showed how different approaches need to be taken when investigating the very fast (relativity) and the very small (quantum mechanics).[5]

It should be noted that heliocentrism did not automatically supplant an earth-centered view of the universe, even among scientists. The theory needed explanation, supplied eventually by Isaac Newton who worked out how gravity applied to all objects, including the sun and the planets, providing mathematical formulas that could be applied to the motion of heavenly bodies. The explanatory power of Newton's system helped refine heliocentrism to the point where it became simpler that Ptolemy's system, as well as a more accurate explanation of observed phenomena. The need to confirm ideas with evidence, to find mechanisms (such as Newtonian mechanics) that informed arguments into which evidence could fit, as well as preference for simpler explanations over more complex ones, defined a new approach to science, the impact of which would extend far beyond the embrace or abandonment of any particular theory.

Philosophy would play an important role in the emergence of this new approach to science. If the walls between science and religion were porous from the Renaissance through the Scientific Revolution and Enlightenment,[6] the distinction between science and philosophy during this period was nonexistent. Indeed, for most of modern history those working in scientific fields were referred to not as "scientists" but as "natural philosophers."

One of these was René Descartes, a philosopher and mathematician who made major contributions to algebra and geometry, both cornerstones of mathematics and science today, as well as kicking off modern philosophy through his mental experiments based on "radical doubt." These inquiries started by questioning the reality of everything, including his own sense perceptions, to determine what was left that could be said to be unquestionably true. His answer, that he was a thinking being (leading to the famous *Cogito,* "I think therefore I am"), was based on the argument that in order for him to engage in thought at all he had to exist as a thinking being. Descartes extended his

For most of modern history those working in scientific fields were referred to not as "scientists" but as "natural philosophers."

ideas into the realm of science in works like *Discourse on the Method for Rightly Directing One's Reason and Searching for Truth in the Sciences* that tried to ground science in the sort of certainty associated with mathematical proofs.

Other philosophers, such as Francis Bacon and David Hume, took a different approach, stressing empirical evidence over abstract reasoning as the source of genuine knowledge. This debate between idealists like Descartes and empiricists like Hume echoed ancient arguments between followers of Plato, who looked to reason as the source of truth with mathematics as their ideal, and those of Aristotle who took the evidence-based field of biology as their model.

It is beyond the scope of this book to show how later philosophers, such as Immanuel Kant, helped bridge this divide (see "Additional Resources" for more information on the history of science, as well as the Renaissance and Enlightenment), but from the examples already mentioned you can begin to see how concepts born from philosophy, such as the central role of evidence, the need for explanation (in the form of mechanisms and models), and skepticism as a means to advance knowledge helped give birth to a new form of scientific inquiry.

Today, students across the world are taught an approach that emerged from these debates under the name the Scientific Method. Using this technique, you pose a question, propose an answer to it (called a "hypothesis"), and then hold the hypothesis as tentative while you gather evidence to support or disprove it. Hypotheses that withstand such scrutiny become "theories" that, while still not declared to be forever and unquestionably true, are considered a strong enough foundation to use as a basis for further inquiry.

Modern science, which features elaborate experiments carefully designed to test hypotheses and formal peer-review in which scientists examine empirical evidence generated by other scientists, attempt to replicate their experiments and findings, and approach explanations and models in the spirit of constructive skepticism, is where this form of reasoning is most advanced. While one can question whether the scientific method we teach school children fully captures the "scientific attitude"[7] that drives such explorations, as well as dig more deeply into questions raised by modern philosophers of science about limitations to today's scientific approaches,[8] for purposes of understanding critical thinking we can utilize common understandings of the Scientific Method to see how such a method can help us gain understanding beyond the realm of science.

Are we taught, or raised, to hold conditional beliefs, put them to honest tests, and stand ready to reject them if they do not conform with facts and observations, regardless of the subject under consideration? Deciding whom to vote for does not require costly and complex equipment, after all, any more than choosing which car to buy requires a formal peer review process. But a critical-thinking approach to these subjects does require you to not jump to an answer but to propose one, test it for reasonableness, and reach a conclusion based on the results of those tests. Such an approach can be described as "thinking like a scientist," but it would be more accurate to say that all critical thinkers, including scientists, rely on methods that, while inspired by the development of modern science, are relevant to every aspect of life.

By the nineteenth century, new disciplines were built around scientific practices that had developed over the previous four centuries, including a science of the human mind: psychology. The nineteenth century was also the time when a new school of philosophy—Pragmatism— was born, and both psychology and Pragmatism play important roles in the creation of the concept of critical thinking.

Psychology and Pragmatism

Critical-thinking researcher Emily R. Lai, citing the work of R. J. Stenberg, contrasted the role of psychology in the development of models of critical thinking with roles played by philosophy and science, pointing out that psychologists "tend to focus on how people actually think versus how they could or should think under ideal conditions."[9]

Psychology as a distinct field emerged in the late nineteenth century, a period when, as just mentioned, many new academic disciplines were created and defined along scientific lines. During this period, Sigmund Freud popularized the notion that our minds are divided, with emotion and animal instinct constantly battling our reasoning selves for dominance. Much of Freud's work has been questioned—even ferociously attacked—as unscientific and even unethical, but his insights, many of them drawn from literary, philosophical, and religious texts, continue to shed light on the rational and nonrational aspects of our mental makeup.

While less well known than Freud in today's popular culture, Germany's Wilhelm Wundt is considered the father of modern, scientific psychology who supplemented traditional philosophic speculation on the makeup of human consciousness with experimental methods drawn from scientific fields such as physiology. By combining measurements of subjects' responses to stimuli with feedback from those subjects, collected through carefully constructed interviews, he created methodologies that still form the basis of contemporary psychological research. France's Pierre Janet played a similar role in the use of scientific methods to study the mind. One of his major contributions was a hierarchy of mental "tendencies" that

While less well known than Freud in today's popular culture, Germany's Wilhelm Wundt is considered the father of modern, scientific psychology ranged from lower-level cognitive activities common to both lower animals and man to higher-order faculties possessed only by humans, such as language and symbolic reasoning.

In the United States, the American professor William James—brother of author Henry James—wrote *The Principles of Psychology* in 1890, one of the most influential psychology texts of its time, while also teaching Harvard University's first courses in psychology.

In addition to the important role he played in the study of psychology based on scientific principles, James was also a pivotal figure in American philosophy who popularized a school of thought called Pragmatism (considered the only major school of philosophy to originate entirely in the United States), the development of which he credited to the brilliant but eccentric Charles Sanders Peirce.

Pragmatism holds that things are defined by their practical effects rather than their empirical or metaphysical properties. A knife is sharp, for example, not because of the width of its cutting edge or participation in some Platonic form of sharpness. Rather, it is our practical use of the knife (to cut something, for example)—and that alone—that defines it as sharp. Similarly, a painting is beautiful because of its aesthetic impact on people, rather than any innate qualities of the work.

The role Pragmatic philosophy played in the genealogy of critical thinking derived from Peirce's Pragmatic analysis of thinking itself, which he saw not as a property of mind or soul, but rather as a means to an end.

Peirce laid out these ideas in one of his few published works: the 1877 *Popular Science Monthly* essay "The Fixation of Belief,"[10] which proposed that doubt motivates all our thinking and that all of us constantly generate beliefs large and small to dispel the discomfort of doubt. With this premise in place, the author described four ways those beliefs can become fixed in our minds.

One is an *a priori* method, which simply requires believing or continuing to believe things that make you comfortable. Alternatively, one's beliefs can be established by an *authority*, such as a priesthood or norms of a society, that establishes what thoughts and ideas are allowed and forbidden. Such authority is often challenged by free spirits, many of whom come to their beliefs through *tenacity*, which involves settling onto a belief system and boldly holding on to it at all costs regardless of whether it is right or wrong.

While all three of these methods for fixing belief (*a priori*, *authority*, and *tenacity*) have something to recommend them, none are great bets as exclusive methods for getting to the truth. If that is your goal, Peirce proposes science as a model, which treats beliefs as conditional even as more and more experiments are performed, and evidence amassed to get us closer and closer to ideas likely to be true.

While Peirce and James played major roles in American intellectual history, it fell to another Pragmatic philosopher working in the field of education, John Dewey, to build these insights into the first concrete incarnation of critical thinking.

John Dewey

John Dewey taught at the University of Chicago and then Columbia University in New York from the 1890s until 1930 and is considered to be one of the most important public intellectuals of the twentieth century. Like William James, Dewey was a Pragmatic philosopher and a major contributor to early theories of human psychology.

It was in education, however, that Dewey is most well-known today. His progressive educational model, which held that students should learn through discovery-based activities rather than explanations by teachers and rote drills, placed him among other educational pioneers like Maria Montessori of Italy and Rudolf Steiner of Austria, whose ideas still influence Montessori and Waldorf schools around the world.

Debates between progressives and advocates for traditional methods for educating children have continued from Dewey's time until today.[11] While thinkers like Dewey, Montessori, and Steiner disagreed on issues like the age students should be taught how to read, what united progressives was the belief that children's minds should not be treated as blank slates to be written on by authority figures. Rather, they should be seen as inquisitive engines capable of creating their own understanding as teachers provided guidance rather than all the answers.

Much of Dewey's work, including the major role he played in politics throughout the twentieth century, reflected his profound belief, bordering on religious faith, in democracy. But a democratic society requires citizens who can take a leading role in their own lives and government by, among other things, being informed and knowing how to approach problems systematically and logically.

Dewey's most famous work, *Democracy and Education*,[12] spelled out how the American education system could be organized to create such democratic citizens. But to understand what he expected such citizens to do, one first needs to look at his earlier 1910 work *How We Think*.[13]

How We Think is grounded in a psychological insight, drawn from Pragmatic ideas first articulated by Peirce, that sees thinking as a means to the end of dispelling doubt, doubt being a mental state that creates visceral pain that people will do anything to eliminate.

The desire to rid oneself of doubt explains the behavior and incomparable learning ability of infants and toddlers whose natural curiosity leads them to use any available faculty—touch, movement, language—to make sense of the world around them.

But, as Peirce noted in "The Fixation of Belief," doubt can be dissipated in numerous ways, some less constructive than others. For example, doubt can be eliminated by believing the first explanation one receives, by embracing ideas one is already comfortable with, or by accepting answers provided by authority figures.

Dewey's problem with the factory model of education of his (and our) day, where teachers provide answers and ensure students learn them and only them through drill and examination, was that this form of learning stifled discovery, which he believed should be facilitated through "overt and exertive" student learning activities. The problem, as he described it in *How We Think*, was that "if activities are admitted at all into the [traditional] school, the admission is a grudging concession to the necessity of having occasional relief from the strain of constant intellectual work or to the clamor of outside utilitarian demands upon the school."[14]

At the same time, Dewey criticized progressive educators who saw discovery-based activity as an end in itself: "At the other extreme is an enthusiastic belief in the almost magical educative efficacy of any kind of activity, granted it is an activity and not a passive absorption of academic and theoretical material."[15]

Dewey answered critics who saw activity-based learning as unstructured and undisciplined by defining characteristics for activities that led to effective learning, in contrast to less thoughtful implementations of progressive principles that assumed the inherent superiority of any activity that did away with elements of the conventional teacher-centered classroom.[16]

Effective learning activities, according to Dewey, begin by providing students with instances that created motivating doubt in their minds, such as ill-defined problems without obvious solutions, especially on topics of interest to individual children. Once such doubt has been instilled, the teacher's responsibility is to channel the students' attempts to dispel that doubt in logical ways.

Dewey did not use the word "logic" to describe the formal logical systems developed by thinkers from Aristotle to Dewey's philosophical contemporaries. Rather, in *How We Think* the term referred to the science-inspired method of reasoning that proposes a solution but holds it to be tentative until evidence has been gathered and tests performed that confirm or disprove one's first attempt at an answer. If disproven, a chain of similar mental experiments continues, ultimately leading to deep and permanent learning.

Dewey termed this mode of reasoning "reflective thinking," summed up as "active, persistent, and careful consideration of any belief or supposed form of knowledge in the light of the grounds that support it and the further conclusions to which it tends."[17]

While other authors would eventually substitute "critical" for "reflective," Dewey provided the first of many definitions for critical thinking you will encounter in this book, and all subsequent work on the subject can be seen as a dialog with ideas first proposed in *How We Think*.

Advances in Understanding of Education, Human Development, and Behavior

Dewey put his ideas into practice (or, more in keeping with his belief system, put them to the test) at the University of Chicago Lab School, a still-extant K–12 institution he helped found.

Like Montessori and Waldorf schools, K–12 institutions such as the Lab School built around progressive educational practices influenced but never supplanted factory models for public education during the twentieth century, a time when public school systems worldwide were expanding to accommodate greater numbers of students from ever more diverse backgrounds. But just as Dewey's ideas would percolate among educators for the next century, the concepts in *How We Think* would continue to develop and be supplemented by input from diverse fields that influence todays' definitions and approaches to critical thinking.

Some of this work came from other academics working in education. This included Edward Glaser, whose 1941 dissertation for Teachers College at Columbia, "An Experiment in the Development of Critical Thinking," created one of the first multifaceted definitions of critical thinking. Glaser's definition included three components: "(1) an attitude of being disposed to consider in a thoughtful way the problems and subjects that come within the range of one's experiences, (2) knowledge of the methods of logical inquiry and reasoning, and (3) some skill in applying those methods."[18] In that same year, Glaser and a Teachers College professor, Goodwin Watson, published the Watson-Glaser Tests of Critical Thinking (a test that still exists today as the Watson-Glaser Critical Thinking Appraisal), which built on Watson's earlier work on assessing complex mental attributes.[19]

Another tool designed to apply scientific principles to how we think was Bloom's taxonomy, published in 1956, which organized educational objectives into a hierarchy of levels of mental complexity.[20] Originally invented to support teachers working in a US higher education system managing rapid postwar expansion, the taxonomy found wide application inside and outside the United States at all grade levels.

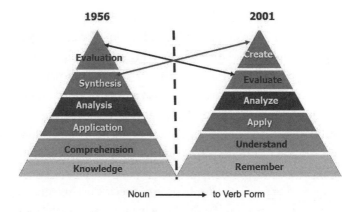

1956 **2001**

Noun ───────► to Verb Form

Figure 1 Courtesy of Leslie Owen Wilson (2001). https://thesecondprinci
ple.com/teaching-essentials/beyond-bloom-cognitive-taxonomy-revised/

As illustrated above, the original version of Bloom's taxonomy began with "Knowledge" at the bottom of the hierarchy, followed by "Comprehension," "Application," "Analysis," "Synthesis," and "Evaluation." A 2001 update, also shown above, put "Creation" (or "Create") at the top of the list, as well as making other additions and modifications that reflected new thinking about how humans develop, learn, and process information.

If the blank-slate model of the human mind was fraying by the beginning of the twentieth century, by mid-century it had completely fallen apart as psychologists shed new light on how our brains develop and work.

In developmental psychology, for example, researchers like Switzerland's Jean Piaget were learning through the long-term study of children that human physical, emotional, and mental development takes place in discrete stages, highlighting the utility of cultivating specific capabilities in young people at the appropriate stage in their growth.

The twentieth century was also a time when advances in surgical techniques and medical technologies provided direct access to the workings of the organ behind all thinking, critical or otherwise: the human brain. The ability of surgeons to save patients with severe brain injuries, for example, helped isolate the purpose of specific brain regions, allowing scientists to study the behaviors and capabilities of those who lost function in one or more of those regions. Similarly, advances that allowed doctors to keep patients safer longer created opportunities to monitor brain activity while a patient was on the operating table.

Over the decades, less invasive medical technologies such as magnetic resonance imaging (MRI) and electroencephalogram (EEG) analysis gave researchers the ability to "see" physical and electrical activity in the brain as it performed tasks. Like developmental psychology, the new field of brain science provided key insights—such as the physical processes involved with memory encoding and retrieval—that would play important roles in understanding how we think.

Research into the workings of the brain also helped inform teaching methods built around the evidence of how our brains seem to work. For example, while Dewey saw great success in activities that required students to build on information and ideas they already understood, research on memory formation provided scientific evidence for the efficacy of building on prior learning.[21]

Two pioneers who contributed additional valuable insights into human mental functioning were the Israeli psychologists Daniel Kahneman and Amos Tversky, whose groundbreaking research in the 1960s and 1970s cast doubt on the effectiveness and stability of reason itself.

Since Aristotle's time, it was generally assumed that reason sets human beings apart from other animals. Based on such an understanding, irrational human behavior was attributed to our emotions or primitive animal instincts overwhelming reason. But, as Kahneman and Tversky demonstrated through a series of intriguing experiments, our reasoning is flawed in several significant ways.

As it turns out, the human mind does not apply the full force of reason to every situation but instead takes shortcuts to more efficiently manage the flow of information coming from our senses and turn that information into understanding upon which decisions can be based. These shortcuts, called "heuristics," likely resulted from natural selection. For example, primitive humans who believed without convincing evidence that a rustle in the bushes signified a nearby predator would have had an evolutionary advantage over those who decided the situation needed further examination before choosing to flee or stay.

The human mind does not apply the full force of reason to every situation but instead takes shortcuts to more efficiently manage the flow of information coming from our senses and turn that information into understanding upon which decisions can be based.

But these same heuristics create biases that can cause reason to fail. For example, as Kahneman describes in his best-selling book *Thinking Fast and Slow*, one such bias called the "Anchoring Effect"

> occurs when people consider a particular value for an unknown quantity before estimating that quantity. … If you are asked whether Gandhi was more than 114 years old when he died you will end up with a much higher estimate of his age at death than you would if the anchoring question referred to death at 35. If you consider how much you should pay for a house, you will be influenced by the asking price. The same house will appear more valuable if its listing price is high than if it is low, even if you are determined to resist the influence of this number. … Any number that you are asked to consider as a possible solution to an estimation problem will induce an anchoring effect.[22]

Other examples include the *availability heuristic* which can bias people toward making choices based on comparisons that come easily to mind. For instance, someone's choice of which college to attend might be influenced by a recent conversation with a friend about his or her experiences at that school more than detailed comparisons researched much earlier. The *effect heuristic* associates experiences with emotional states—often unrelated to the experience itself. For instance, one might be more inclined to buy a lottery ticket based on having had recent happy or sad experiences, rather than the odds of winning or losing on that particular day.

The biases that derive from these heuristics might seem like mental equivalents to optical illusions,[23] but with regard to critical thinking they are anything but innocent. To take the most obvious example, "Confirmation Bias," the human tendency to accept information that conforms with our existing beliefs and reject information that contradicts those beliefs, can be seen as the primary cause for many of the irrational behaviors and acts of tribalism that plague the planet today.

The presence of biases means being able to think critically requires more than just understanding mental tools such as logic and the skills developed by putting those tools to use. It also requires us to understand the prejudices our reasoning is susceptible to and train ourselves to reflect on and control for those shortcomings.

Turning Point?

A "Big Bang" moment in the teaching of critical-thinking skills in higher education came in 1983 when the California state university system required all students to complete a critical-thinking course before graduation, one that would help them develop "an understanding of the relationship of language to logic, leading to the ability to analyze, criticize and advocate ideas, reason inductively and deductively, and reach factual or judgmental conclusions based on sound inferences drawn from unambiguous statements of knowledge or belief."[24] Packed into that requirement were enormous assumptions regarding what constituted quality thinking skills, as well as an implication that such skills could be taught.

Proponents of the California legislation, which included a diverse set of actors forming a loose "Critical Thinking Movement,"[25] hoped that the new initiative would inspire other states to create similar requirements for graduation. Although few states followed California's lead, the decision led to a nation-wide expansion of critical-thinking courses in higher education. That expansion created hundreds of new sites for experimentation in critical-thinking teaching, as well as an ever-increasing body of research on critical-thinking education, from the 1980s onward.

Nineteen eighty-three was also the year that President Ronald Reagan's National Commission on Excellence in Education published the enormously influential report *A Nation at Risk*.[26] The study viewed the American education system as falling behind those of other countries, putting at risk, among other things, our nation's economy and military security. As a result of the commission's work, improving schools through accountability practices centered on rigorous academic standards and regular assessments of student learning became a new national priority.

As with many topics in this chapter, a full rundown of the policy initiatives triggered by *Nation at Risk*—from George W. Bush's "No Child Left Behind" to Barack Obama's "Race to the Top"—and of the controversies still swirling around overreliance on standardized testing is beyond the scope of this book. But just as the "age of achievement"[27] triggered by *Nation at Risk* defined decades of educational policy, discussions of critical thinking and other "twenty-first-century skills" like communication and collaboration have become key policy points informing the development of subject-based standards such as the Common Core.

Underlying many of the educational transformations described above, which were paralleled in educational policy discussions around the globe,[28] was the move from an industrial to a knowledge-based economy that prioritized skills such as the ability to reason effectively, communicate persuasively, and work cooperatively over the ability to assimilate and regurgitate raw information. As raw knowledge has become increasingly accessible with a simple mouse-click or phone swipe, members of an "Information Age" society need to know how to make effective use of that knowledge by thinking more clearly—and critically—about it.

Orphans

In 1892, a group of educators dubbed "The Committee of Ten" led by Charles Elliot, president of Harvard, recommended a standardized curriculum for elementary grades through high school built on subjects like reading and writing, math, and science (broken into a sequence of subfields like physics and chemistry) that still informs the structure of K–12 education in the United States and around the world.[29] This structure provided homes for the many new subjects covering vast fields of knowledge, especially scientific knowledge, generated from the Renaissance on. But it also created orphan subjects such as logic and rhetoric that had formed the backbone of previous education models.

Subjects like logic have not been completely banished from the curriculum. Courses dedicated to it are still taught at many, if not most, institutes of higher education, and, if we define computer programming as the heir to Aristotle's original logical systems, practical applications of logic are being studied by more students today than ever before.

That said, the act of critical thinking requires one to understand a number of ideas inspired by the events and advances described in the intellectual and educational history presented in this chapter. Critical thinking is also a skill built on that body of knowledge, meaning the elements that comprise it must be practiced before critical thinking can be used effectively in situations where an informed decision would likely produce the most beneficial results. Critical thinking also requires the development of habits that inspire a person to follow a path of critical thinking versus finding some shortcut to dispel doubt that can lead to error—such as believing everything you are told.

While debate continues over what should be included in the list of knowledge, skills, and dispositions required to think critically, there is enough consensus among those who study and teach critical thinking to inform a discussion of what's in and what's out. That is the subject we shall turn to in the next chapter.

COMPONENTS OF
CRITICAL THINKING

Now that you are familiar with where the concept of critical thinking originated, it is time to take a look at what one should know and be able to do in order to become a critical thinker.

A review of critical-thinking research literature, or even a simple Google search, will provide a host of hierarchies, taxonomies, and diagrams that describe and illustrate the knowledge, skills, and personal attributes a critical thinker should possess. Even within these sometimes-overlapping, sometimes-competing descriptions, however, there is a set of elements that appears consistently enough to consider as the consensus components of critical thinking.

This chapter will look at these consensus components, such as structured thinking/logic, language skills, and argumentation, as well as introduce some additional skills

and attributes, such as creativity and personal dispositions, that a growing number of researchers and educators
believe are necessary to think critically.

Structured Thinking

I chose the phrase "structured thinking" over the word
"logic" to highlight the fact that different methods for
structuring our thinking exist and that disciplining ourselves to think in an organized fashion is more important
for critical thinking than which method we choose. That
said, the critical thinker's debt to logic is profound since
each of the following systems for structured thinking is
built on a logical foundation to accomplish the same goals:

Making clear what we or others are thinking or
communicating

Making transparent the reasons behind what we believe
or want others to believe

Having the ability to determine if reasons for belief are
justified

Definitions and Distinctions
Before introducing specific logical systems, keep in mind
that these systems tend to fall into two broad categories.

The first, *formal logic*, focuses on the structure of arguments, and many varieties of formal logic provide powerful symbolic representations of statements and ideas that have proven incredibly useful (just ask any logician or computer programmer). In contrast, *informal logic* looks at both the structure of arguments and the meaning of the words within them in order to apply logical principles to everyday communication.

While formal logic, including many systems invented over the last two centuries, provides new ways of looking at contemporary and age-old problems,[1] critical-thinking instruction tends to focus on informal logic, exemplified by the name of the American association of critical thinking educators: The Association for Informal Logic and Critical Thinking (AILACT).[2]

Both formal and informal logic use a set of common terms, including:

Argument—A set of statements that provide evidence in support of a conclusion

Premise—A statement of evidence in an argument

Conclusion—The claim in an argument that the arguer is asking to be accepted as true if the premises are true

Inference—Steps in logical reasoning leading from the premises to the conclusion

Logical Form—The abstract structure of an argument, which can be expressed symbolically, separate from the words that make up the argument

Validity—The quality of an argument that "takes a form that makes it impossible for the premises to be true and the conclusion nevertheless to be false."[3]

Soundness—The quality of an argument in which the premises are true and the logical form is valid

Making use of these definitions, another distinction to keep in mind is one between *deductive* and *inductive* reasoning. Deductive arguments are "self-contained" in that everything needed to determine whether the conclusion is true can be found in the premises and the form that the argument takes. The term "valid" refers to a deductive argument that requires you to accept the conclusion as true if you accept the premises as true. Similarly, a deductive, valid argument in which the premises are *actually* true is said to be sound.

With inductive arguments, accepting the premises as true can provide support that the conclusion is likely to be true, rather than must be true. In contrast to the all-or-nothing nature of deductive arguments that are valid or not, inductive arguments can be evaluated on a continuum of strength and weakness. This can be based on the probability of the conclusion being true and the acceptability, relevance and sufficiency of an argument's premises.[4]

The fact that inductive arguments are, by definition, invalid (since you can always find a counter-example that lets you accept the premises as true, but still reject the conclusion) might make you think that deductive reasoning is superior to inductive. Yet many, if not most, of the arguments we are exposed to in everyday life are inductive rather than deductive. For instance, debates over what to do in the future—such as changing a tax code or buying one brand of dishwasher over another—almost always include premises or a conclusion that describe something that has not yet happened, making them unprovable until after a decision resulting from the argument is made.

Even science, which represents one of the most successful applications of reasoning in human history, relies primarily on inductive reasoning. An argument that the sun will come up tomorrow, for instance, is based on high probability rather than certainty, given that the sun has come up every day in recorded history. Similarly, when Sherlock Holmes "deduced" this or that conclusion from available evidence, he was more often than not using inductive reasoning to determine the most likely explanation for what he observed.

With these definitions and distinctions in mind, let's look at methods and examples of logical reasoning, starting with systems created by Aristotle.

Aristotle's Syllogisms

As mentioned in the last chapter, Aristotle invented the first widely used system of logic, one that became the basis for teaching the subject for centuries.

The cornerstone of his system was the *syllogism*, an argument made up of three (and only three) statements: two *premises* (the things you are asking someone to accept as true) and the *conclusion* (the statement you are saying someone must believe is true if they accept the premises as true).

In a syllogism, both premises and the conclusion must be written in one of the following ways:

All P's are Q's (called an *A statement*)

No P's are Q's (called an *E statement*)

Some P's are Q's (an *I statement*)

Some P's are not Q's (an *O statement*)

Here is a simple example:

Premise 1: All <u>dogs</u> are *animals*

Premise 2: All **collies** are <u>dogs</u>

Conclusion: Therefore, all **collies** are *animals*

Note that these statements are written in a specific form consisting of a major premise (the first statement), a minor premise (the second statement) and the conclusion (the last statement). The major premise includes the *major term* (in *italics* in the example above) which appears in one premise and serves as the predicate of the conclusion. The minor premise includes the *minor term* (in **bold**) which is also in one premise and appears as the subject of the conclusion, while a *middle term* (underlined) appears in both premises but not in the conclusion.

In this example, both premises and the conclusion are A statements (i.e., written in the form "All P's are Q's"). Based on Aristotle's system, any argument written in the proper form, with correctly structured major, minor and middle terms, which consists only of A statements (called an AAA syllogism) is *valid*, meaning that accepting the premises as true requires you to accept the conclusion as true.

You can test this yourself by asking if there is any way you can accept that the premises ("All dogs are animals" and "All collies are dogs") are true but still reject the conclusion that "All collies are animals" by coming up with a counterexample that lets you accept the premises but still reject the conclusion. If, as in this example, you cannot, then the logic behind this valid syllogism is airtight.

As it turns out, there are 256 different combinations of A, E, I, and O statements that can be built into a three-statement syllogism written in proper form, only twenty-four of which produce valid arguments. This means not only that our AAA syllogism involving collies is valid, but that any syllogism with correctly structured major, minor and middle terms that has the AAA structure is also valid. And if the premises of those valid arguments are actually true, the arguments are sound.

Syllogistic reasoning provides a mechanical way to distinguish valid arguments from invalid ones. In fact, for centuries students of logic were taught all kinds of songs, poems, and other mnemonic tricks to memorize which types of syllogisms led to validity. This made logical analysis a process of translating a spoken or written argument into the three properly structured statements of a syllogism and then determining whether that structure fit one of the twenty-four valid cases.

While Aristotle's system represented a major intellectual breakthrough, later developments, such as propositional logic, provided additional logical forms capable of expressing valid arguments that could not be addressed by the Aristotelian syllogism, such as those with more than two premises.[5]

Other Logical Forms
Two other valid logical forms that emerge frequently in logical argumentation are *modus ponens* and *modus tollens*.

Modus ponens arguments take the general form:

Premise 1: If P, then Q

Premise 2: P

Conclusion: Therefore, Q

In this case, the first premise sets up a general condition with the second premise establishing whether this condition has been met or not.

An example of a real-world modus ponens argument would be:

Premise 1: If it's raining, the ball game will be called off.

Premise 2: It's raining.

Conclusion: Therefore, the ballgame will be called off.

Here is a more famous argument (at least among logic teachers), one that dates back to at least the fourteenth century C.E.:

Premise 1: All men are mortal.

Premise 2: Socrates is a man.

Conclusion: Therefore, Socrates is mortal.

Rewritten in modus ponens form, the argument would read:

Premise 1: If Socrates is a man, then Socrates is mortal.

Premise 2: Socrates is a man.

Conclusion: Therefore, Socrates is mortal.

This is another example of a valid deductive argument in which accepting the premises as true requires you to also accept the conclusion as true. As with all valid arguments, if the premises of the argument are actually true, then the argument is sound.

Another example of a valid logical form is modus tollens, which has this symbolic structure:

Premise 1: If P, then Q

Premise 2: Not Q

Conclusion: Therefore, Not P

An example of a modus tollens argument would be:

Premise 1: If Erica graduated college, she would have a diploma.

Premise 2: Erica does not have a diploma.

Conclusion: Therefore, Erica did not graduate college.

As with our modus ponens examples, this modus tollens argument is valid. It can be challenged, for example, by questioning whether having or not having a diploma is required to establish whether someone graduated college (perhaps pointing out that if Erica lost her diploma, that wouldn't negate her having graduated college). But this challenge targets the truth of one of the premises (Premise 1), not the inference that connects the premises to the conclusion. If we could demonstrate that having a diploma is not required to establish college graduation, that would show that the argument, while still valid, is unsound (since one of its premises is false).[6]

Real World Examples

The simple examples you just read are the kinds you might see in a logic or critical-thinking textbook. But the reason logic is so integral to thinking critically about the world is that everyday communication can often be broken down into premises and a conclusion that fits one or more logical forms. For example, assume you're at a dinner party and someone makes this statement:

> Multinational organizations are dangerous! Any self-respecting country should stop funding them immediately. They reek of corruption, are a huge waste of taxpayer money, and are a threat to a nation's self-determination.

With a bit of massaging, this dialog can be turned into the following syllogism:

Premise 1: All self-respecting countries are entities that should not fund organizations that are corrupt, a waste of taxpayer money, and a threat to a nation's self-determination.

Premise 2: All multinational organizations are corrupt, a waste of taxpayer money, and a threat to a nation's self-determination.

Conclusion: All self-respecting countries are entities that should not fund multinational organizations.

The argument can also be translated into modus ponens form as:

Premise 1: If an organization is corrupt, a waste of taxpayer money, and a threat to a nation's self-determination, self-respecting countries should not fund them.

Premise 2: Multinational organizations are corrupt, a waste of taxpayer money, and a threat to a nation's self-determination.

Conclusion: Self-respecting countries should not fund multinational organizations.

Note that with both forms of the argument, accepting the premises as true requires you to accept the conclusion as true, making the arguments valid. However, one of the premises in each form of the argument—the one that implies that all multinational organizations are corrupt, a waste of taxpayer money, and a threat to a nation's self-determination—can easily be refuted by providing a single example of a multinational organization that does not have one of those three negative characteristics. Thus, our dinner party argument condemning multinational organizations is valid, but unsound.

Turning everyday arguments into structured forms exposes the reasoning behind them, providing an opportunity to evaluate whether or not the argument provides sufficient reasons to believe the conclusion. As you just saw in the analysis demonstrating how our dinner party argument is unsound owing to one of its premises being false, the words making up the argument also provide information for analyzing the quality of an argument.

Informal logic methods that allow you to write the premises and conclusion of an argument using real-world language provide flexibility for everyday use of logical principles, which is why informal logic plays such an important role in the teaching of critical thinking. For example, let's say that in response to the original argument noted above, someone says this:

That's ridiculous! I work for a multinational organization and every dollar we get from governments is spent on helping people, so we are not corrupt at all. And the money donated to groups like ours buys good will around the world. So multinational organizations benefit, rather than hurt, countries that fund them.

This can be turned into the following structured argument.

Premise 1: The multinational organization I work for spends every dollar on helping people.

Premise 2: Organizations that spend all their money on helping people are not corrupt.

Premise 3: Money donated by countries to the multinational organization I work for buys donor countries good will.

Premise 4: Being involved with an organization that buys donors good will benefits donor nations.

Conclusion: Contributing to multinational organizations benefits, rather than hurts, countries that fund them.

In this case, the argument has four premises and each premise and the conclusion are written in language that is easy to understand. But, like the syllogism, this less-confined argument can also be tested for validity by asking yourself: "If I accept every premise as true, do I have to accept the conclusion as also true?" In this case, it is easy to come up with a way to accept the premises and reject the conclusion—for example, you could claim that even if the premises are true for one multinational organization, that doesn't mean all such organizations are similarly virtuous.

This can be solved by adding one more premise, implied in the original argument but not stated outright, to make the argument valid:

Premise 1: The multinational organization I work for spends every dollar on helping people.

Premise 2: Organizations that spend all their money on helping people are not corrupt.

Premise 3: Money donated by countries to the multinational organization I work for buys donor countries good will.

Premise 4: Being involved with an organization that buys donors good will benefits donor nations.

Premise 5 [Hidden premise]: All multinational organization are just like the one I work for.

Conclusion: Contributing to multinational organizations benefits, rather than hurts, countries that fund them.

Aristotle called hidden premises *enthymemes* and teasing out such unstated premises is one of the most productive steps in argument analysis, since the most important point of an argument is often implied but not stated directly. For example, arguments over whether abortion is a surgical procedure or murder rests on the often-unstated premise of whether a fetus is a human being.

Getting back to our example, with the addition of the hidden premise, the argument becomes valid, requiring you to accept the conclusion as true if you accept all of the premises as true. In order to be sound, however, every premise in this valid argument must *actually* be true, or at least something a reasonable person would accept as plausible.

In the response argument above in favor of multinational organizations, for instance, the premises involving the arguer's personal experience might be difficult to challenge without substantial research. But it is easy to challenge the just-added, originally hidden fifth premise by simply finding one example of a corrupt multinational organization. This would make the new premise easy to reject, and if even one premise in a deductive argument fails, then the entire argument, while still valid, is unsound (and thus no good).

This same method can be used to structure and evaluate inductive arguments, which, as mentioned earlier, do not require you to accept the conclusion as true just because you accept the premises as true. For example, if further on in the discussion of funding for multinational organizations someone said:

> Well, funding for multinational organizations is widely popular among the public and there does not seem to be any majority in the legislature against it. Given that the government has increased spending on multinational organizations every year since it has been in office and that this year's budget includes another increase, I'd say the government will be spending more on them this year than last year.

That would translate into the following four-premise argument:

Premise 1: The government has increased spending on multinational organizations every year since it has been in office.

Premise 2: This year's budget includes an increase in spending for multinational organizations.

Premise 3: There is no majority in the legislature opposed to an increase in spending for multinational organizations.

Premise 4: Support for spending on multinational organizations is widely popular among the public.

Conclusion: The government will spend more on multinational organizations this year than last year.

In this case, one can find a way to accept the premises as true, but still reject the conclusion as false. One such counterexample would be a scenario in which a minority stalls legislation to increase spending on multinational organizations despite the majority and public support. This makes the argument invalid, but because this is an inductive argument, rather than a deductive one, we are looking for whether or not the conclusion is likely to be true if the premises are true. Because it is very likely that the conclusion is true if the premises are true, the inferences leading from the premises to the conclusion can be described as strong, although the argument as a whole would be weakened if it turns out that one or more of the premises were false.

Fallacies

Bad arguments are often "broken" or flawed in similar ways. These frequently occurring errors are called *fallacies*, and many critical-thinking courses focus considerable time and attention on teaching students to spot fallacious reasoning in everyday arguments.

Some flaws relate to the structure of an argument. For example, Woody Allen in his *War and Peace* parody film *Love and Death* gave us this variation on our previous Socrates argument:

Premise 1: All men are mortal.

Premise 2: Socrates is a man.

Conclusion: Therefore, all men are Socrates.

This example fails because the form of the argument is incorrect. In a properly structured argument, the major term (in *italics*), minor term (in **bold**) and middle term (underlined) would be organized like this:

Premise 1: All <u>men</u> are *mortal*.

Premise 2: **Socrates** is a <u>man</u>.

Conclusion: Therefore, **Socrates** is *mortal*.

Notice that in Woody Allen's version, the middle term (men/man) appears in both premises and the conclusion. This is called the *fallacy of the undistributed middle*, and arguments with this form fail (i.e., are invalid) for the same structural reason.

Another fallacy, called *denying the antecedent*, is an invalid logical form with the following structure:

Premise 1: If P, then Q

Premise 2: Not P

Conclusion: Therefore, not Q

Sticking with the modus ponens version or our Socrates argument, an invalid version that commits the fallacy of *Denying the Antecedent* would read:

Premise 1: If Socrates is a man, then Socrates is mortal

Premise 2: Socrates is not a man

Conclusion: Therefore, Socrates is not mortal

In this case, it is simple to come up with a counter-example in which Socrates is not a man, but still mortal. For example, Socrates could be the name of someone's pet goldfish, which would make Premise 2 true, but would not lead to the conclusion being true.

A similar fallacy, called *affirming the consequent*, is based on this invalid form:

Premise 1: If P, then Q

Premise 2: Q

Conclusion: Therefore, P

An example of an argument that commits this fallacy would be:

Premise 1: If Torrance gambled away all his money, he would be broke

Premise 2: Torrance is broke

Conclusion: Therefore, Torrance gambled away all his money

As with other invalid arguments, it should be obvious that the conclusion does not follow from the premises, given that there are any number of ways to explain how Torrance could have gone broke without gambling away all his money. This is to say that there are many possible counterexamples in which the premises are true, but the conclusion false.

Fallacies stemming from structural flaws like the three you just read are called *formal fallacies*. Recalling the distinction between formal and informal logic, *informal fallacies* are problems that arise owing to the content rather than the structure of an argument. For example, claiming that Byzantines are criminals because Jethro the Byzantine was just arrested for armed robbery commits the *composition fallacy*, mistakenly attributing characteristics of a member of a group to the entire group. Another informal fallacy, the *association fallacy*, commonly referred to as "guilt by association," is committed by the person who accuses her neighbor of being a vandal because her brother's wife's mailman was caught throwing a rock through a store window.

While those last two examples might seem frivolous, fallacious reasoning is far from benign. Bigoted statements that condemn entire races for the behavior of a few members or public figures hounded from office for the conduct of one of their Twitter followers (or follower's followers) are examples of the harm these flawed ways of thinking inflict on the world.

Given the complexity of language, and the diversity of human interactions in which language is used, informal fallacies can take a number of forms. For example, they could appeal to something other than reason such as fear (*appeal to the stick*) or popularity (*appeal to the people*). Fallacious arguments can also be based on drawing a conclusion from too little information (a *hasty generalization*) or by presenting a false choice or *false dichotomy* such as "either you pass my budget or millions will starve."

A number of fallacies also attempt to distract a reader or listener from the specifics of the argument, by attacking the arguer (called *ad hominem*) or presenting an oversimplified or distorted version of an opponent's argument and attacking this parody, rather than the actual argument (a *straw man* fallacy). Some of these informal

Fallacious reasoning is
far from benign.

logic errors demonstrate challenges in determining when an argument is actually fallacious. For example, in some cases attacking the person making an argument represents an *ad hominem* fallacy, but in other instances challenging an opponent's character might be justified (if he or she has been convicted of perjury, or simply has a history of lying).

Lists of fallacies that appear in books and on websites (including those listed in Additional Resources) number in the hundreds, with the vast majority of fallacies being informal rather than formal. This indicates that as much or more can go wrong with the content of an argument as with the argument's structure. This is why, in the study of critical thinking, it is valuable to consider principles drawn from both formal and informal logic.

Drawing Things Out

Our toolkit for determining the quality of arguments need not be limited to words. For instance, Venn diagrams similar to the ones elementary school students are taught when they learn about sets can be used to map out statements in an argument, such as in figure 2.

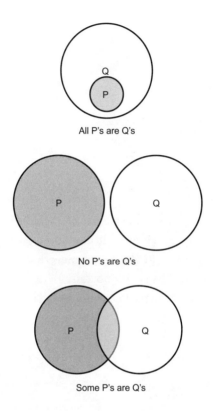

Q

P

All P's are Q's

P

Q

No P's are Q's

P

Q

Some P's are Q's

Figure 2

These relationships can be combined to illustrate complete arguments, such as our Socrates example, as seen in figure 3.

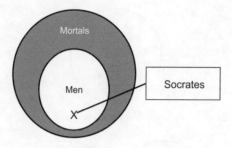

Figure 3

In this case, the impossibility of Socrates being a man but not being mortal is visually illustrated by the inclusion of Socrates (the X) in the set of men that is completely contained within the set of mortals.

Our first cocktail party argument can be similarly represented as in figure 4.

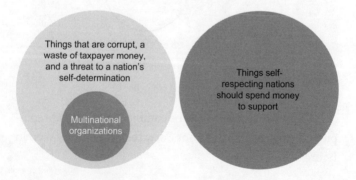

Figure 4

In this case, there is no overlap between the set of things that are corrupt, a waste of money, and a threat to a nation's self-determination and the second set of things that self-respecting nations should spend money to support. Since the set of multinational organizations falls completely into the first set (at least in our admittedly unsound argument), there is no way that a subset of corrupt, wasteful, threatening things (multinational organizations) can intersect with a set of things self-respecting nations should spend money supporting. This provides a graphical demonstration that we are dealing with a valid argument.

Another popular method of representing arguments visually was developed by British philosopher Stephen Toulmin. Rather than starting with premises leading to conclusions, *Toulmin diagrams* begin with *grounds* leading to a *claim*, which can be illustrated as in figure 5.

The arrow going from the grounds box to the claim box illustrates that the grounds must lead to or provide evidence to support the claim. If we use Toulmin's method

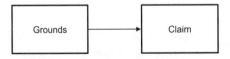

Figure 5

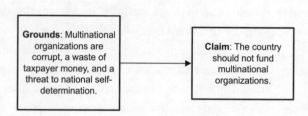

Figure 6

to map out our cocktail party argument, it would look like in figure 6.

The link between the grounds and the claim must itself be justified in a Toulmin diagram through another element called a *warrant*. Continuing with our example, the argument with a Warrant included would look like in figure 7.

At first glance, this type of diagraming might not seem to add much to previous ways of breaking down a logical argument if you simply consider grounds as another word for "premise" with the claim serving as the conclusion and

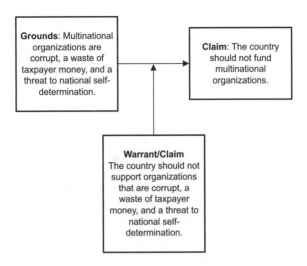

Figure 7

the warrant providing the reasoning linking the two. But notice how this form of argument diagraming requires you to more explicitly spell out the logical inference between a premise and conclusion (or grounds and claim) in the form of the warrant, a link not always spelled out so clearly in an argument form represented only with words.

Once this logical link is exposed, it can serve as another point of analysis or attack by creating a new branch of the argument in which the original warrant does double duty as the warrant for one branch of the argument and the claim for a new branch, as in figure 8.

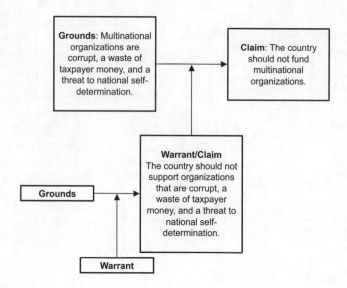

Figure 8

This ability to branch out to include multiple lines of reasoning is another advantage of diagraming arguments, since doing so allows you to capture the dynamic sorts of interchanges that take place in real-world debates that might go in multiple directions.

Another technique for illustrating arguments that is a bit easier to grasp than Toulmin's method (which makes it popular with young learners) is the *argument map*, which is used below to illustrate the rebuttal to our cocktail party example argument, as seen in figure 9.

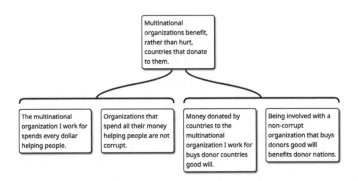

Figure 9

In this map, the conclusion at the top (also called the *main claim*, which highlights how the claim an argument is asking you to accept as true if the premises are true does not always come at the end of the argument) is supported by two lines of reasoning. On the left side, the first two premises work together (which make them *co-premises*) to provide a single reason to support the main claim, as do the second two premises on the right. Like Toulmin diagrams, argument maps provide a means to illustrate complex arguments that branch out horizontally and vertically. Unlike Toulmin's more complex system, this technique allows you to analyze arguments by asking the same simple question of every part of the argument: Does what appears in a box below provide reasons to believe what appears in the box above?

These examples provide a glimpse into the wide range of alternatives that support structured thinking, with more information on these and other logical systems appearing in the Additional Resources section of this book. The tools and methods you can use to understand and analyze arguments are diverse, and if you are interested in teaching critical thinking or becoming a critical thinker yourself, there is no right or wrong choice regarding which system you use or invent. The only option not on the table is leaving your thinking unorganized.

Language Skills

Since humans are not machines that communicate entirely through formally structured statements, a critical thinker must be skilled at translating normal human language into the premises and conclusion that make up a structured argument so that those statements can be used as the basis for logical analysis.

Translation

You have already seen examples of translation, such as our cocktail party debate where everyday dialog had to be boiled down to a set of premises leading to a conclusion by eliminating extraneous wording and turning vague language associated with normal human conversation into clear statements that fit the structured format to which logical rules can be applied.

Since the rules of logic, once internalized, often become second nature, much of the work of critical thinking involves translating everyday human communications such as editorials, advertisements, or persuasive discussions into clear, structured language. Like any other translation process, there is an art to boiling complex communication to its logical essence, which is why the ability to perform this type of translation is a critical-thinking skill that requires significant practice.

Machines cannot perform this translation task as yet, any more than they can turn Russian novels into Japanese with one hundred percent accuracy. But even if logical translation cannot be done by algorithm, there are some principles critical thinkers performing such translations should follow.

Translations should be accurate.—Errors can enter the translation process in different ways. One of these, intentional error (the deliberate misreading of someone else's words or misleading presentation of one's own thoughts), fails the test of charity I'll be describing shortly. But even unintentional errors that occur as a result of ignorance can lead to misunderstanding an argument. For instance, if someone interpreted "multinational organizations" in our example arguments

Much of the work of critical thinking involves translating everyday human communication into clear, structured language.

as "multinational for-profit corporations," that would lead them to misunderstand arguments that are most likely about multinational nongovernment organizations and charities, such as the United Nations or Amnesty International.

Translation should be economical.—Not all logical translations require a reduction of words. You have already seen one example where the addition of words in the form of a hidden premise (an enthymeme) is necessary for an argument to make sense.

Given the importance of making our words clear, however, simplicity that respects accuracy should always be the goal. Excluding unnecessary statements from our argument (like "That's ridiculous!," which expresses emotion but adds no substance), is one way to simplify an argument, as is choosing the fewest words needed to accurately capture points that originate in more verbose and potentially vaguer prose.

Economy also involves trying to capture an argument in the fewest number of premises possible. Given what you now know about the tests for validity and soundness, the virtue of economy should make sense. One bad premise is all it takes to declare a deductive argument unsound or weaken an inductive one, so having fewer premises reduces the potential for one or more of them failing.

Since we are talking about simplicity, I would also like to note a relevant philosophical principle called *inference to the best explanation*. This principle provides guidance when dealing with questions that cannot be definitively answered, such as whether God exists or whether we are all characters in a novel being written by an alien living in an alternative universe.[7] Matters like these cannot be solved empirically (through sense perception or by performing experiments), but different answers to these types of questions can be argued and more likely options chosen over others.

In general, inference to the best explanation prefers simpler explanations over more complex ones. For instance, accepting the alien novelist theory mentioned above requires us to believe in two universes. In contrast, not accepting it requires us to believe in only one (the one we perceive), which makes it the preferred choice, even absent evidence. Among philosophers, this approach to explanation has triggered more than a century of discussion and debate over what can be known and the nature of belief. For purposes of becoming a critical thinker, however, the message is simpler: streamline as much as possible without sacrificing accuracy.

Translations should be charitable.—The philosopher Nigel Warburton provides this example of what philosophers call the *principle of charity*:

In a debate about animal welfare, a speaker might state that all animals should be given equal rights. One response to this would be that that would be absurd, because it would be nonsensical, for example, to give giraffes the right to vote and own property since they would not understand either concept. A more charitable approach would be to interpret the claim "All animals should have equal rights" as being a shorthand for "All animals should have equal rights of protection *from harm*" and then to address that.[8]

On the surface, this might just seem like an alternative version of our call to be accurate, but the principle of charity goes beyond just honest translation, asking us to engage with the strongest version of an argument rather than intentionally weakening it through an uncharitable translation.

One need only look at the fights that routinely break out in the comment sections of news or social media sites, where debaters pounce on grammatical or typographical errors, or argue with parodies of their opponent's positions, to see what lack of charity can do to civil discourse. But the benefits of charitable behavior go far beyond helping the translation process.

To start with, engaging with the strongest possible version of an opponent's argument, rather than harping on a nonvital flaw or finding some other way to debate a

The principle of charity goes beyond just honest translation, asking us to engage with the strongest version of an argument rather than intentionally weakening it through an uncharitable translation.

weaker version, allows you to stretch your mental muscles, just as athletes gain more by competing with strong rather than weak opponents. In many cases, strong arguments have flaws and vulnerable points, but engaging first with their strengths facilitates more robust and honest engagement with ideas, versus the fallacy-filled free-for-alls you see in those aforementioned internet "debates."

The process of charitable translation requires you to act as if you were going to present your logical translation of another person's argument to that other person and ask them if you properly and honestly captured what they were trying to say before proceeding to debate the topic. Such a process requires *empathy*, the ability to enter the mind of another person to discover what they believe and why they believe it. In addition to facilitating more honest discussions, such empathy also turns out to be a powerful control for confirmation bias, the human mind's tendency to accept things that conform to what we already believe and reject things that do not, a flaw in our reasoning that makes us all vulnerable to misunderstanding and manipulation.

Persuasive Communication

Speaking of manipulation, one other set of language-related skills relevant to critical thinking involves persuasive communication, historically referred to as *rhetoric*.

Rhetoric, if you recall, was one of the subjects Aristotle organized and codified in his book on the subject, which pointed out that there are ways of communicating in writing or in speech that have a powerful impact on audiences, regardless of the subject being communicated. Some of these rhetorical devices, such as alliteration (repeating of an initial constant sound, as I did when I just described "fallacy-filled free-for-alls") or rhyming move readers and listeners, whether those devices are used in poems, songs, or political speeches.

Beyond these familiar literary techniques, there are a number of rhetorical devices that are particularly good at making oratory compelling. One such device is *anaphora*, the intentional repetition of words for effect. For example, when presidential candidate Hillary Clinton appealed to "my supporters, my champions ... my sisterhood!" those extra "my's," which might seem awkward when read, made the spoken version of this phrase more compelling. That same statement is also an example of the rhetorical device *tricolon,* which caps part of a speech with a group of three words or phrases, groups of three being particularly effective in speechmaking. Another example, *chiasmus*, is the intentional switching of word order within a phrase or sentence, best exemplified by John F. Kennedy's still-remembered inaugural show-stopper "Ask not what your country can do for you, ask what you can do for your country."

There are also rhetorical techniques for structuring a speech or other presentation by starting with a folksy, ingratiating opener (called an *exordium* in Latin) and building to a fiery crescendo (called a *peroration*). Every presidential address you have ever seen likely used these techniques, which can be traced back to ancients like Aristotle and the Roman orator Cicero, demonstrating that rhetoric is not just powerful but timeless.

The role rhetoric should play in critical thinking is a point of debate, likely because most critical-thinking teachers are professional philosophers or at least trained in philosophy, and the animosity between the schools of philosophy and rhetoric goes back to the Golden Age of Athens.

When Socrates defined philosophers as "lovers of wisdom," he was partly motivated to set them apart from another group called the sophists. The sophists were traveling teachers who would instruct the wealthy and ambitious in verbal tricks that could make communication more effective, that is, persuasive. In democratic Athens, moving audiences such as juries in court or a governing assembly was the key to power. Because of this, helping people master a crowd became a lucrative business. But the sophists' willingness to help others learn to make weak arguments seem stronger put them in the crosshairs of philosophers who sought genuine truth above the mere appearance of truth.[9]

Despite the twenty-five hundred years of controversy between philosophy and rhetoric, understanding the role of rhetoric in human communication can advance the cause of critical thinking. To begin with, many of the extras that may need to be cut from prose arguments to distill them into clear, unambiguous premises and conclusions are likely to be rhetorical devices designed to persuade (like the aforementioned "That's ridiculous!") but not necessarily inform. This makes understanding the nature of persuasive language helpful in determining what might belong in a logical argument and what can be discarded.

Also, if rhetoric can be used to make a weak argument seem stronger, understanding rhetoric provides a critical thinker with the "X-ray vision" needed to pierce the verbal fog and find the poor reasoning or false premises behind it.

Finally, if rhetoric can make a bad argument seem more persuasive, imagine what it can do for a good one. Even if your premises are true and the logical inferences linking them to your conclusion solid, you still need to get people to pay attention to what you are saying. Tying your valid, sound, strong (and ideally moral and ethical) arguments to persuasive techniques that have been moving audiences for centuries can make them not just convincing but unstoppable.

Tying your valid, sound, strong (and ideally moral and ethical) arguments to persuasive techniques that have been moving audiences for centuries can make them not just convincing but unstoppable.

Argumentation

A fallacy I failed to mention earlier is *equivocation*, which arises from confusion (intentional or accidental) that results from many words having more than one meaning. A word you have read several times in this chapter that has multiple meanings is "argument."

In one sense, an argument can be defined as a set of statements that include evidence (in the form of premises), a conclusion, and logical inferences connecting the premises to the conclusion. By this definition, an Aristotelian syllogism, taken as a whole, can be considered a single argument, as can the cocktail party arguments you have seen rendered in different forms.

But argumentation can also be defined much more broadly, with one researcher describing it as encompassing "both the expression of ideas, thoughts, feelings and suppositions; the joining together of these ideas and notions in logical and quasi-logical sequences, supported (usually and beneficially) by evidence; and also the positioning of the student in relation to existing bodies of knowledge."[10] Based on this definition, a complex "argument" between advocates of different policy positions might include several linked logical "arguments" made by each party participating in the debate.

Depending on how broadly one defines the term, one could make the case that critical thinking is entirely about argument generation and analysis, and many critical-thinking courses tend to emphasize argumentation in their syllabi. But given that definitions of critical thinking have broadened to include a range of noncognitive components, including personal traits like curiosity and open-mindedness, it is better to think of the mastery of argumentation as a vital component of critical thinking but not synonymous with it.

Of the several "lay" dictionary definitions of argument, the ones most relevant to the critical-thinking project include "a coherent series of reasons, statements, or facts intended to support or establish a point of view"[11] or "a form of rhetorical expression intended to convince or persuade."[12] These definitions capture the essential goal of argumentation in critical thinking: to justify belief in something for yourself or to get others to embrace an idea or change their minds.

These definitions contrast with another familiar understanding of "argument" as "an angry quarrel or disagreement."[13] This is the negative-leaning definition that tends to come to mind when people first think about arguments, associating the word with shouting matches between family members, political adversaries, or patrons at a bar.

The presence of heated language does not necessarily mean that argumentation based on our critical-thinking definition is not taking place. The methods one uses to get people to change their minds might include drama or charged rhetoric. But we should be careful to distinguish genuine, if loud, arguments from a different sort of activity: fighting.[14] In fighting, winning and getting your way takes precedent over convincing someone to change their beliefs.

The use of physical coercion is a telltale sign that a fight and not an argument is taking place. Using violence to get people to do what they are told does not require anyone to change their mind but only to change their behavior to avoid a beating. Other ways to get your way without honest persuasion include blackmailing someone (including moral blackmail) or just raising the emotional temperature of a confrontation so high that people will do whatever it takes to escape an uncomfortable situation, regardless of what they believe.

Given that the goal of critical thinking is to find reasons to support beliefs, activities like fighting that provide only reasons to avoid physical or emotional pain fall outside the definition of argumentation used by reflective thinkers. While appeals to emotion should not be off-limits to a genuine critical thinker arguing an issue, thoughtful acts of persuasion should be measured and focused on getting others to want to believe what you are telling them.

There are other forms of communication that do not involve argumentation or fighting. Sports listings in the newspaper, for example, provide a set of facts, rather than reasons to believe something, making them an *explanation*, rather than an argument. The distinction between an argument and an explanation can be subtle. A weather report, for example, generally provides facts but might use those facts to support predictions, in which case those facts serve the role of premises in an argument with one or more predictions serving as the argument's conclusion. As one philosopher summed up the distinction: "The act of explaining is designed to increase the audience's comprehension, the act of arguing is aimed at enhancing the acceptability of a standpoint."[15]

Background Knowledge

While many important exercises in logic are based on abstractions (such as variables in statements like "If P, then Q" in which P and Q can stand for different things), critical thinking, with its focus on informal reasoning, tends to be applied to some subject. So, knowledge of the relevant subject is a vital component of most critical-thinking exercises.

The degree to which reasoning is bound up with the content reason is being applied to is summed up by Daniel T. Willingham, University of Virginia professor of cognitive psychology, who provides these examples:

Educators have long noted that school attendance and even academic success are no guarantee that a student will graduate an effective thinker in all situations. There is an odd tendency for rigorous thinking to cling to particular examples or types of problems. Thus, a student may have learned to estimate the answer to a math problem before beginning calculations as a way of checking the accuracy of his answer, but in the chemistry lab, the same student calculates the components of a compound without noticing that his estimates sum to more than 100 percent. And a student who has learned to thoughtfully discuss the causes of the American Revolution from both the British and American perspectives doesn't even think to question how the Germans viewed World War II. Why are students able to think critically in one situation, but not in another? The brief answer is: Thought processes are intertwined with what is being thought about.[16]

Looked at through the lens of the logical structures you were just introduced to, facts can be seen as forming or informing the premises of an argument supporting a conclusion. Just as creating premises requires understanding subject matter, critiquing those premises for errors or weaknesses also requires being knowledgeable about their content.

Information Gap

In the next chapter, you will read about the role of background knowledge in debates over where and how critical-thinking skills should be taught. Before addressing that issue, however, we need to consider a question that pervades discussions of background knowledge in the Internet Age: What does access to knowledge mean in an era when, for many people, a large percentage of that knowledge is just a few phone swipes or mouse clicks away?

The disparity of technological resources between rich and poor, including rich and poor nations, is one element of this new information gap, which is really an access-to-information gap. This inequity can involve equipment such as computers, smartphones, and other devices. Regarding access to information, however, these devices do not become useful until they are hooked into the internet, which makes the availability of high-speed internet connections, free from government control, another vital technology chasm to be closed.

Without minimizing the equity issues just cited, even technology "haves" face a daunting problem: how to navigate this universe of ever-expanding data (much of it true and valuable but too much of it false or irrelevant) to find the right information, evaluate its quality, and make appropriate use of it.

Information Literacy

This brings us to another modern skill that can be considered an increasingly important component of critical thinking: information literacy. This field emerged in the 1970s, the same era when the similar field of media literacy developed to help students and the public understand how to evaluate content provided by traditional media sources such as newspapers, radio, and television. Outside of these forms of widely available media, the primary source for information beyond the home was the public or academic library, which explains why the field of information literacy emerged from the discipline of library science.

The library has historically been the place where expensive and hard-to-obtain sources of information, such as diverse collections of books, periodicals, and journals, were collected and made available to specific communities like students enrolled at a university or the public at large. Once new media, such as microfilm, databases on CD ROMs, and online information sources became available, the library continued to be the place where these valuable, often expensive resources could be accessed by anyone with a library card.

As librarians continued to support increasingly complex and technically sophisticated sources of information, they reinvented their profession, turning from book and manuscript collectors and preservers into information specialists. The field of information literacy they created provides a framework for approaching information everyone needs today as those sources expanded exponentially and entered our classrooms, homes, and workplaces via ever-present computers and mobile devices.

At a high level, information literacy "is the ability to identify what information is needed, understand how the information is organized, identify the best sources of information for a given need, locate those sources, evaluate the sources critically, and share that information. It is the knowledge of commonly used research techniques."[17] Those who are "information literate" understand and apply the following steps:

Locating information—This step includes strategies for finding the highest-quality sources using diverse techniques that go beyond simple web searches.

Evaluating information—This step involves applying a set of tests to analyze information for quality in terms of, among other things, accuracy, relevance, and timeliness.

Organizing information—This step brings order to collections of information, an order that helps make it possible to determine patterns or that makes the information more useful for a specific task (like writing a research paper).

Synthesizing information—This step employs the information gathered, evaluated, and organized to

Information literacy provides a framework for approaching information everyone needs today as information sources expanded exponentially and entered our classrooms, homes, and workplaces via ever-present computers and mobile devices.

accomplish tasks such as answering questions or creating "work products" like the aforementioned research paper.

Communicating information—This step involves sharing what has been created, for example, answers to questions or papers, with others where that information can become part of an information ecosystem navigated by those with information literacy skills.

A trip to the now-familiar Additional Resources section will help you learn more of the nuts and bolts of each of these steps and about information literacy in general.

What is important to remember is, whether your background knowledge comes from printed words or digital sources, whether it emerges from years of studying a subject or quick online research adequate for a particular purpose, when it comes to critical thinking the bottom line is you cannot think critically about a subject if you don't know what you're talking about.

Creativity

If critical thinking were only about facts and logic, creativity might seem out of place as a core critical-thinking skill. As you saw in the last chapter's discussion of the latest version of Bloom's taxonomy, however, creativity (represented by the verb "create") now sits atop the pyramid—in other words, it represents the highest of higher-order thinking skills. Anyone who has struggled to build an elegant logical proof or chemical derivation would likely argue for the important roles imagination and creative qualities and activities play in such intellectual efforts.

The widespread use of creativity in the critical-thinking process also makes sense in the context of the approach to problem solving described by John Dewey in *How We Think*. This approach involves proposing a hypothesis, testing it, rejecting the hypothesis if those tests fail, or accepting it conditionally if the hypothesis survives testing.

While clearly systematic, the process Dewey describes —one inspired by science but applicable to all projects requiring reflective thinking—also has a creative element. For where are the hypotheses to be tested and the experiments to test them to come from if not from someone imagining possibilities that may not have been proposed or tested before?

Scientists, after all, do not draw their ideas solely from facts or observations. They also look for patterns or devise experiments that might force new patterns and observations to the surface. Like any form of artistry, the search for patterns that might not be obvious or the development of something new, whether a painting or a scientific experiment, is fundamentally a creative act.

In recent decades, the role of design in the success of popular products like Apple's iPhone has inspired interest in design-based processes in areas as diverse as business and education, with "design thinking" serving as a catch-all term for increasingly popular experiment-based, iterative approaches to knowledge formation, discovery, and "making."[18] Attempts to include the arts—including practical arts like design—in what were once thought of as solely scientific and mathematical disciplines are also what turned STEM (science, technology, engineering, and mathematics) into STEAM (with the added "A" representing arts).[19]

One way to consider the role of creativity in critical thinking is to see it as providing new material to which structured reasoning (provided by the other critical-thinking tools you've been reading about) can be applied—in this case material that might initially exist only in the imagination. As Dewey wrote over a century ago in *How We Think*:

> The imaginative stories poured forth by children possess all degrees of internal congruity; some are disjointed, some are articulated. When connected, they simulate reflective thought; indeed, they usually occur in minds of logical capacity. These imaginative enterprises often proceed thinking of the close-knit type and prepare the way for it. In this sense, a thought or idea is a mental picture of something not actually present, and thinking is the succession of such pictures."[20]

Dispositions

In the discussion so far, I have introduced you to characteristics that a critical thinker should possess—such as curiosity, empathy, and creativity—that might seem more at home in a personality profile than a curriculum or set of academic standards. These terms relate to human *dispositions*, also called attributes or behavioral traits, that describe what a person practicing critical thinking should demonstrate when applying the knowledge and skills associated with disciplined reasoning to real-life situations.

As critical-thinking classes proliferated, especially in higher education starting in the 1980s, teachers involved with those courses and researchers working in the field of critical-thinking education identified a wide range of the dispositions needed to not just think effectively and reflectively but to be willing to put that ability into practice, especially in situations where thoughtful reflection might not be a person's only choice or first instinct.

The Foundation for Critical Thinking, a California-based US nonprofit founded in the 1980s, has been a major force in developing support for critical-thinking education in the United States.[21] The foundation's work has included developing frameworks that articulate what it means to be a critical thinker, including a set of "valuable intellectual traits" similar to many other lists of the personal characteristics a critical thinker should possess.[22] The foundation's list includes the following attributes:

Intellectual humility—Recognition of the limits of your knowledge, as well as of potential flaws in your own reasoning

Intellectual courage—The ability to argue for your beliefs confidently and not passively accept what you are being told is true, even in the face of social pressure

Intellectual empathy—A willingness to put yourself into the mind of others to better understand their positions

Intellectual autonomy—Thinking for yourself, while maintaining control over your own reasoning

Intellectual integrity—The ability to think and argue honestly, holding yourself and others to the same rigorous intellectual standards, as well as a willingness to admit when you are wrong

Intellectual perseverance—Readiness to put in the hard intellectual labor needed to overcome obstacles in order to answer questions or argue one's positions

Confidence in reason—Belief that, over time, everyone is best served by adherence to reason as the best means to gain knowledge and find solutions to problems

Fairmindedness—Putting in the good-faith effort to treat all viewpoints fairly, regardless of one's own beliefs, emotional reaction to issues being discussed, or community norms (such as peer pressure to agree with a single point of view)

Note that this set of dispositions encompasses many aspects of the human condition beyond the intellectual, including emotional, ethical, and social aspects of our makeup. As such, we can use dispositions, working separately and together, to define what it means to be a critical-thinking person. For instance, intellectual humility (which asks us to respect our limitations) and intellectual courage (which requires us to stand up for our beliefs when we feel the reasoning behind them is justified) can serve as two poles between which a golden mean balances characteristics to define an intellectual virtue.[23]

These dispositions also have ethical dimensions. Empathy and fairmindedness, for example, are intellectual variations on the view that you should treat others as you want to be treated, a spirit also captured in the "Golden Rule" morality of reciprocity associated with nearly all religious and ethical traditions. Similarly, intellectual integrity, like any form of integrity, presumes there are a set of ethical absolutes that should govern everyone's choices equally.

We can use dispositions, working separately and together, to define what it means to be a critical-thinking person.

The foundation's list of intellectual traits is one of many generated by educators and researchers to define the full set of dispositions that a critical thinker should possess. In fact, so many different sets of intellectual virtues have been generated over the decades that additional effort has been needed to try to gather them into a comprehensive collection that consolidates characteristics traveling under different names, such as *inquisitiveness* and *curiosity*, or words and phrases that might represent different aspects of the same concept, such as *respect for alternative viewpoints* and *open-mindedness*.[24]

As you will read about in the next chapter, there is considerable discussion over how to work critical-thinking education into existing primary, secondary, and postsecondary school systems. But even if an embrace of critical thinking as an educational priority gives topics like logic and argumentation a new place of prominence in the educational ecosystem, it is not clear where, how, or even whether the kind of "morals education" associated with teaching intellectual virtues would fall within such a regime.

Out of Many, One

While the purpose of this book is not to pick favorites, either among alternative lists of virtues or competing definitions of critical thinking, it is worth noting an important consensus, one shared by nearly everyone working in this field, that critical thinking consists of three interconnected parts:

Knowledge—Including knowledge of components of critical thinking such as logic, language, and argumentation

Skills—The ability to put those components of critical thinking to use in real-world situations

Dispositions—The personal characteristics needed to prioritize reasoning over other ways of learning or making decisions, the willingness and readiness to put the tools of critical thinking to use, and the commitment to use one's critical-thinking ability honestly and ethically

Implied in this and any other attempt to define or explain critical thinking is the expectation that a critical thinker is aware of what is going on in his or her own head. This makes *metacognition*, the awareness and understanding of one's own thought processes, another skill a critical thinker needs to develop, and willingness to reflect on one's own thinking another disposition that should be part of a critical thinker's makeup.

While the role that core skills like logic play in improving reasoning might be obvious, the role of noncognitive attributes like open-mindedness and empathy can also be viewed as vital tools required to reason well.

To understand why, consider the insights drawn from psychology mentioned in the last chapter, including one we all know from our own life experience: that the human mind is divided into warring parts that include reason, emotion, and instinct. Also, the individuals that possess these divided minds interact with other individuals as part of some social system. To make matters even more complicated, even when we try to bring our reason into play to make thoughtful choices not driven by emotion or social pressure, human reasoning turns out to be flawed, and thus susceptible to error and manipulation resulting from biases that might be hard-wired into our brains.

While some have argued that the nature of our minds makes it difficult if not impossible for people to ever behave rationally, the intellectual virtue of confidence in reason provides us with the disposition to look for and reflect on reasons for rational beliefs, rather than simply believe what we are told or fall prey to errors in thinking to which everyone is prone. Similarly, other dispositions provide powerful methods for controlling emotions, instinct, or biases that can lead our thinking astray.

Open-mindedness, for example, means willingness to be open to ideas with which one disagrees. Emotion might create visceral discomfort in having to think about (or even listen to) opposing viewpoints, while confirmation bias makes it easier to accept evidence and arguments supporting one's viewpoints over those contradicting them. But by maintaining an open mind, one is in the position to learn more about views one does not currently hold.

Such open-mindedness needs to balance the ability to identify and reject unreasonable arguments, such as crank race theories or proposals for perpetual-motion machines, with the disposition to not treat every argument you disagree with as the equivalent of a conspiracy theory. Properly internalized, open-mindedness could lead you to change your mind about something you thought you believed or provide you with insights needed to convince others to change their beliefs. Open-mindedness on the part of both participants in an argument or larger groups—including society as a whole—might lead to new answers and ideas that were not apparent to anyone before he or she participated in a deliberative process driven by the knowledge, skills, and dispositions associated with critical thinking.

From this optimistic viewpoint, critical thinking might provide solutions to many of the problems we face—from politics driven by tribalism and negative emotion to environmental or economic catastrophes created or made worse by irrational ways of thinking about them. Before exploring the benefits that critical thinking might bring to individuals or the world, however, we need to address the challenges that stand in the way of making the development of critical-thinking abilities a centerpiece of education, if not society as a whole. This is the subject I turn to next in a discussion of how critical thinking can be defined, taught, and assessed.

DEFINING, TEACHING, AND ASSESSING CRITICAL THINKING

So far, you have read about the origins of critical thinking as a distinct concept and how increasing our ability to reason well became an important societal goal and educational priority. You also learned about knowledge, skills, and dispositions many researchers and educators have identified as being required to become a critical thinker.

Since few people would argue against the need for more critical thinking applied to the world's problems, most discussions about the subject among educators, employers, and policymakers are over how to achieve needed increases in critical-thinking ability. The previously mentioned analysis that says more than three quarters of employers believe the graduates they hire lack this crucial ability, one that almost all teachers and professors claim to be prioritizing, represents a gap to explore as we look at important issues surrounding the ways critical thinking can be defined, taught, and assessed.

Can Critical Thinking Be Defined?

When introducing the genealogy of critical thinking, I mentioned how attempts to define the term have shed light on a number of important matters, ones that relate directly to how (or even whether) critical thinking can be taught and assessed.

Differing Definitions

Lack of a consensus definition does not mean no one has any idea what you are talking about when you mention "critical thinking." Rather, there are many competing definitions developed at different times that focus on different priorities.

You have already encountered some attempts to define the term, including John Dewey's 1910 definition of reflective thinking as "active, persistent, and careful consideration of any belief or supposed form of knowledge in the light of the grounds that support it and the further conclusions to which it tends," as well as Edward Glaser's 1941 multifaceted description of critical thinking as "(1) an attitude of being disposed to consider in a thoughtful way the problems and subjects that come within the range of one's experiences, (2) knowledge of the methods of logical inquiry and reasoning, and (3) some skill in applying those methods."

These definitions are echoed in the 1983 California requirement that all graduates of state colleges and universities complete a critical-thinking course that teaches "an understanding of the relationship of language to logic, leading to the ability to analyze, criticize and advocate ideas, reason inductively and deductively, and reach factual or judgmental conclusions based on sound inferences drawn from unambiguous statements of knowledge or belief."

The Foundation for Critical Thinking, the aforementioned California-based nonprofit that has worked on critical-thinking education for decades, has another definition that incorporates several priorities, including metacognition (thinking about your own thinking) and overcoming bias, which they characterize as arising internally (*egocentrism*) and externally (*sociocentrism*). The foundation defines critical thinking as

> that mode of thinking—about any subject, content, or problem—in which the thinker improves the quality of his or her thinking by skillfully analyzing, assessing, and reconstructing it. Critical thinking is self-directed, self-disciplined, self-monitored, and self-corrective thinking. It presupposes assent to rigorous standards of excellence and

mindful command of their use. It entails effective communication and problem-solving abilities, as well as a commitment to overcome our native egocentrism and sociocentrism.[1]

In a literature review of academic works, Emily Lai, a researcher for the educational publisher Pearson, identifies over a dozen different definitions for critical thinking emerging from the fields of philosophy, psychology, and education.[2] These include

"reflective and reasonable thinking that is focused on deciding what to believe or do"[3];

"thinking that is goal directed and purposive, 'thinking aimed at forming a judgment,' where thinking itself meets standards of adequacy and accuracy"[4]; and

"the mental processes, strategies, and representations people use to solve problems, make decisions, and learn new concepts."[5]

Lai, Matthew Ventura, and Kristen DiCerbo from Pearson, working with the educational nonprofit Partnership for 21st Century Learning, also published a paper titled "Skills for Today: What We Know about Teaching and Assessing Critical Thinking."[6] This document proposes a complete framework for how to think about critical thinking, one that emphasizes measurable skills over harder-to-evaluate dispositions in pursuit of the practical goal of creating curriculum and assessment for critical-thinking education programs.

One of the most widely cited definitions of critical thinking came from a 1990 research study led by Dr. Peter Facione. Dr. Facione worked with forty-six US and Canadian critical-thinking educators, half of whom were associated with philosophy departments and half from the physical and social sciences, to create a consensus definition for critical thinking and the associated practices and qualities necessary to become a critical thinker. This consensus was reached via a structured process for decision-making and forecasting known as the Delphi method, which led to the "Delphi Report,"[7] in which critical thinking was defined as

> purposeful, self-regulatory judgment which results in interpretation, analysis, evaluation, and inference, as well as explanation of the evidential, conceptual, methodological, criteriological, or contextual considerations upon which that judgment is based.

While these definitions vary, and some definitions prioritize certain elements over others, it would be a stretch to say they are so different from one another that no consensus can be reached regarding what critical thinking is. The three-part nature of critical thinking mentioned in the last chapter—knowledge, skills, and dispositions—certainly encompasses most of the definitions listed above.

Some definitions (like Pearson's) prioritize knowledge and skills over dispositions, while others (like that of the Foundation for Critical Thinking) stress individual responsibility for monitoring and improving one's own thinking. Such variability of priorities, however, should be seen as a sign of a healthy debate rather than a crippling lack of definition. The teaching of traditional subjects like language and math also vary and evolve, as attested to by changes in educational standards over the decades, and the elements that fit into various critical-thinking definitions are considerably fewer in number than those making up more expansive fields like biology.

What is "in" or "out" regarding critical thinking is the most substantive aspect of these definitional debates. You have already read arguments as to why certain subjects (or subsets of those subjects) like information literacy, rhetoric, and creativity should be given a home under the mantle of critical thinking. While some might disagree with the extent of their inclusion, they do not threaten the goal of the critical-thinking project: to create autonomous individual actors capable of thinking systematically and independently.

But what about ideas that challenge this goal?

The goal of the critical-thinking project is to create autonomous individual actors capable of thinking systematically and independently. But what about ideas that challenge this goal?

Individual versus Group Thinking

Peter Elbow, professor emeritus of English at the University of Massachusetts, teaches writing via a two-step process. The first consists of "freewriting and fast exploratory writing," which he describes as "the postponing of vigilance and control during the first stage of writing" in favor of open-ended inspiration and exploration of hunches. Only after this unstructured writing process is complete would a writer take a structured approach to his or her work, often through interactive group critiquing sessions modeled on processes associated with group therapy.[8]

Rather than separate these two stages into undisciplined/creative versus structured/critical, Elbow refers to them as first-order and second-order thinking, each with its own benefits and role to play in writing *and* in the general thinking process. In later works, he also developed the idea that critical thinking, which emphasizes finding flaws in one's own thinking or the thinking of others, represents a "doubting game" that needs to be supplemented by a "believing game" in which one tries to find strengths even in seemingly bad reasoning (or writing).[9]

While Elbow's ideas have analogs in conventional critical-thinking practices, such as the role of creativity and the principle of charity, the benefits of second-stage thinking taking place in group settings also point to the idea that thinking might be a social act, something that takes place between people, rather than something occurring entirely in the heads of autonomous individuals. Philosopher Connie Missimer adds that social thinking can provide "an evolutionary view in which terms like good and bad, appropriate or reasonable, and critical thinking are meaningless without historical and social reference points,"[10] highlighting the role social norms might play even for those trying to think autonomously.

The idea that group-based reasoning and decision-making processes can equal or even surpass thinking performed by individuals has precedents—from experiments in democracy over the centuries to the jury system of today. When performing estimates (like guessing how many jelly beans are in a jar), for example, averaging many guesses tends to generate a number closer to the truth than strategies chosen by individuals to determine the right count. Cass Sunstein, coauthor of the book *Nudge*,[11] which advocates channeling certain human cognitive biases toward productive policy goals, also explored group reasoning in his 2006 book *Infotopia: How Many Minds Produce Knowledge*.[12] Inspired by the vast expansion of communication and collaboration capabilities enabled by the internet, Sunstein tried to determine which group dynamics led to superior reasoning and which could cause destructive "group-think."

While the mechanisms behind social thinking are less well understood than the two-thousand-year-old rules of logic, there is clearly a role for communication and collaboration in the critical-thinking process. For definitional purposes, however, pouring whole new (and complex) categories of human endeavor into a critical-thinking bucket runs the risk of overflowing it with elements that might be only partially relevant to the goal of creating critical thinkers.

Bigger Picture
An alternative to adding ever more elements to the critical-thinking construct would be to make critical thinking itself a component of something larger.

One of the most well known attempts to create such a synthesis is the P21 Framework for 21st Century Skills,[13] created by the aforementioned Partnership for 21st Century Learning, which in 2002 organized a coalition of educators, employers, and government leaders to map the full range of skills needed by students in the new millennium. Their complete framework is expansive, including not just thinking skills but approaches to content, pedagogy, and assessment. For purposes of this discussion, however, the P21 framework identifies critical thinking as one of "Four Cs," which include critical thinking, communication, collaboration, and creativity organized as overlapping domains.

The P21 framework identifies critical thinking as one of "Four Cs," which include critical thinking, communication, collaboration, and creativity.

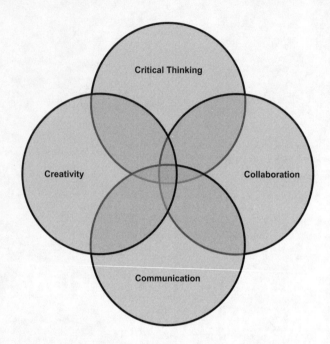

Figure 10

Thinking of these four skills as intersecting versus subsuming each other provides a practical way to understand the roles they may or may not play with regard to one another. For example, an intersection of critical thinking, collaboration, and communication could define the skills needed to participate in social reasoning while leaving room for individual critical-thinking skills outside this intersection. Similarly, an overlap between critical thinking and creativity could include creative activities relevant to reflective and scientific thought, such as conceiving hypotheses and experiments, while still leaving plenty of nonoverlapping space in the creativity circle for skills related to purely artistic endeavors.

A different, and more controversial, expanded framework has been developing as critical analysis gets applied to critical thinking itself. Advocates for this framework acknowledge the importance of the traditional critical-thinking practices such as logic and argumentation, which are associated with what is often called the critical thinking movement, but also see those practices as just one of several steps needed to truly function as a reasoning person.

A subsequent step, often referred to as *critical pedagogy*, owes a debt to modern philosophical movements such as postmodernism and deconstruction that, among other things, ask questions about what we can really know given the limitations of the tools at our disposal, especially language. For example, those associated with the critical thinking movement and those writing about critical pedagogy assign different meanings to the word "critical," as Martin Davies and Ronald Barnett note in their introduction to the *Palgrave Handbook of Critical Thinking in Higher Education*:

> The critical thinking movement theorists had taken the adjective "critical" to mean "criticism,"

(becoming aware of weaknesses in some claim or argument). Their aim was putting logic at the service of clear thinking. The critical pedagogues, by contrast, took "critical" to mean "critique" (i.e., identifying dimensions of meaning that might be missing or concealed behind some claim or belief or institution).[14]

These missing or concealed meanings could include hidden power structures or assumptions so built into a culture's social order that the biases they generate are unnoticeable. Thus, for the critical pedagogue, the duty of the critical thinker is to grasp these assumptions and use that knowledge to expose the hidden structures behind them. Davies and Barnett, in their *Palgrave Handbook* introduction, present further steps that could define this evolving extended pathway, including "critical action," which asks those who have been able to pierce the veil covering aspects of how the world really works to act on that knowledge to change society for the better.

What kinds of assumptions might be hidden behind this veil? Picking one relevant to this book, most of the fields that have inspired critical thinking (classical philosophy, modern science, psychology) and the tools in the critical thinker's toolbox (such as logic and argumentation) originated in Ancient Greece, premodern and modern Europe while "critical thinking" itself is a concept that evolved originally in the United States. Did the work of developing conceptions for "critical thinking" unearth universal truths about human nature, analogous to scientific discoveries about gravity or the atomic nature of matter, or should they be seen as creations of a particular (Western) culture? If it is the latter, might there be effective methods of reasoning from other cultures that should be considered when teaching thinking skills, or might the forms of logic we teach represent cultural creations (or even impositions) rather than universal truths?

In addition to these cultural questions, feminist scholars like Karen J. Warren have written analyses of critical thinking that, like similar critiques of science, ask whether the distinctions, hierarchies, and methods of separating "bad" from "good" evidence and reasoning might represent binary approaches to knowledge generated by institutions such as philosophy, science, or the academy itself, that have been historically dominated by men.[15]

Those more in agreement with critical thinking movement approaches are not ready to have their pedagogy reduced to mechanical logics and argumentation methodologies, especially given their embrace of nonmechanistic categories like creativity, personal dispositions, and ethics. Political agendas chosen by some advocates of critical pedagogy and critical action also leave those embracing more familiar approaches asking whether critical pedagogy and action represent the natural next steps in the evolution of critical-thinking education or attempts to replace the teaching of how to think with what to think.

We will leave these interesting topics here, not because they are politically fraught, but because discussion of them moves very quickly into complex questions of epistemology, the branch of philosophy that asks how we can know anything at all. If you read more about these debates,[16] however, notice that, at least for now, proponents for each side still use the general critical-thinker's toolbox (logic, argumentation, persuasive communication) to present and argue their views.

Can Critical Thinking Be Taught?

As with questions regarding how critical thinking should be defined, debates over teaching critical thinking are less about whether critical-thinking skills can be taught and more about the best approach for doing so. After all, some of the most important elements of critical thinking, such as logic, have been taught for over two thousand years, far longer than almost any other subject that now makes up traditional school curricula. So, discussions over the teaching and learning of critical thinking need to focus on the when, where, and how rather than whether critical-thinking skills are teachable at all.

When to Start

Starting with when, in the best-selling 2015 book *The Teenage Brain: A Neuroscientist's Survival Guide to Raising Adolescents and Young Adults*,[17] Dr. Frances Jensen, professor of neuroscience at the University of Pennsylvania's School of Medicine, brought her professional experience to bear on the task of figuring out the mental growth and behavior of young people, including her two teenage sons.

Through an analysis of research on how parts of the brain develop, work alone, and work together, informed by advances in brain-imaging technology, Jensen highlighted that, just as infancy is a time of massive expansion of cognitive ability in areas such as language and motor skills, adolescence is a period of similar rapid growth in the parts of the brain that control reasoning. While the brain might not grow in mass as children reach this stage of their lives, the synaptic connections between neurons that define brain complexity and govern levels of mental ability continues to expand rapidly, if unevenly, as children become adolescents.

Growth in connections that support reasoning helps explain the rapidly rising ability of young people to debate and argue, whether in a writing assignment for school, a competitive debate, or pleas for a later bedtime or the car keys, as they move from early adolescence to young adulthood. The uneven growth Jensen documents also helps

Just as infancy is a time of massive expansion of cognitive ability in areas such as language and motor skills, adolescence is a period of similar rapid growth in the parts of the brain that control reasoning.

explain why these often-demonstrated reasoning skills do not translate to better judgment in everyday affairs.

Brain development, as it turns out, is "back-to-front," meaning the prefrontal cortex behind our foreheads, which has been associated with decision-making and self-control, is not fully "wired" into other brain parts that govern systematic reasoning until people reach their early to mid-twenties. This helps explain why students can spend a morning acing exams and skillfully arguing their positions in classroom discussions and then engage in risky behavior or make foolish choices in the afternoon.

In addition to helping children and parents better understand behavior patterns that emerge with puberty, these psychological discoveries also indicate that adolescence would be an ideal time to introduce students to structured forms of reasoning and argumentation that take advantage of natural abilities already expanding at this point in their lives.

While research on brain development pinpoints a particular period (secondary school) when the teaching of critical thinking skills might find a receptive audience, there is no obvious lower limit to when children can begin developing their critical-reasoning abilities.

For example, a 2013 study in the United Kingdom discovered that teaching philosophy to primary school students had a positive and dramatic impact on various measures of educational attainment, including in areas such as literacy and math skills, an impact that was particularly pronounced among lower-income learners.[18]

The Philosophy for Children (P4C) program examined in the 2013 study was created by the Society for the Advancement of Philosophical Enquiry and Reflection in Education (SAPERE). It involved getting young students to engage in real philosophical debates over questions such as "What is truth?" or ethical issues like bullying. During an experimental trial, discussions took place once a week (on average) over several months and were led by teachers trained in the P4C methodology.

As described in the research study on P4C that involved over three thousand students in nearly fifty schools, "The aim of the programme is to help children become more willing and able to question, reason, construct arguments and collaborate with others." While the exact mechanisms whereby regular philosophical discussions brought about increased scores for subjects like language and math are not fully understood, the methodologies associated with philosophy—such as making statements clear and finding and articulating reasons for belief—certainly play roles in the teaching and learning of language, math, and all other topics. At the very least, the positive impact the program had on diverse young learners indicates that the teaching of critical thinking can take place in early grades, a goal embraced by public philosophers working to bring philosophy to wider audiences.[19]

Additional studies support the notion that age-appropriate critical-thinking content can support a progression of critical-thinking development throughout the years that children spend in school.[20] Important educational initiatives, such as the Common Core English Language Arts (ELA) and math standards informing the instruction of millions of students in most US states, are built around increased understanding of grade-based developmental progressions.

As an example, the first Common Core ELA writing standard asks students to write opinion pieces in early grades (K–5), which evolve into argumentative writing in grades 6–12. At each grade level, the requirements increase with regard to understanding the logical structure of arguments and evaluating the quality of evidence, progressing to the point where the following twelfth-grade Common Core ELA writing standard might seem at home as a learning objective in a college-level critical-thinking course:

> Introduce precise, knowledgeable claim(s), establish the significance of the claim(s), distinguish the claim(s) from alternate or opposing claims, and create an organization that logically sequences claim(s), counterclaims, reasons, and evidence.[21]

This discussion of academic standards and education approaches brings up another question regarding the teaching of critical thinking: Where in the curriculum should instruction in critical thinking take place?

Where Should Critical Thinking "Live"?

In postsecondary education, where subject-specific courses are taught alongside cross-disciplinary and remedial ones, courses dedicated to teaching critical-thinking skills can be found in the catalogs of many colleges and universities. The University of California system still makes taking a critical-thinking course a requirement for graduation, and, while California's 1983 initiative did not trigger similar requirements in other state college systems, it contributed to a dramatic expansion in critical-thinking courses in higher education, courses frequently (although not exclusively) offered by the schools' philosophy department.

An alternative to creating dedicated critical-thinking courses would be to incorporate critical-thinking instruction into specific subjects like writing, science, and history. This strategy would give teachers trained in those disciplines the ability to integrate the appropriate critical-thinking skills into content students are already learning. That ELA standard for writing argumentative essays quoted above, for example, gives students the opportunity to learn about logical structure and quality of evidence in the context of writing about topics that interest them. Similarly, science teachers teaching the scientific method can combine those insights with critical-thinking pedagogy to show students how hypothesis formation and testing can be applied to any form of inquiry.

In many cases, decisions regarding where critical thinking should be taught are made for practical rather than pedagogical reasons. Colleges and universities, after all, can offer electives that focus on specific topics, a flexibility not available in most public education systems built around traditional subjects (notably language, math, science, and social studies) taught, increasingly, to specific standards at each grade level.

In 1989, Robert H. Ennis, philosopher of education at the University of Illinois, urged educators and researchers to avoid looking at dedicated critical-thinking courses versus the integration of critical-thinking instruction into traditional course material as a binary choice.[22] Rather, he proposed a framework involving four approaches—*general*, *infusion*, *immersion*, and *mixed*—that outlines how critical thinking can be taught:

> By the "general approach" I mean an approach that attempts to teach critical thinking abilities and dispositions separately from the presentation of the content of existing subject-matter offerings, with the purpose of teaching critical thinking. …
>
> *Infusion* of critical thinking instruction in subject-matter instruction is deep, thoughtful, well understood subject-matter instruction in which

students are encouraged to think critically in the
subject, and in which general principles of critical
thinking dispositions and abilities are *made explicit*.
On the other hand, *immersion* is a similar thought-
provoking kind of subject-matter instruction in
which students do get deeply immersed in the
subject, but in which general critical thinking
principles are *not made explicit*. ...

The *mixed* approach consists of a combination
of the general approach with either the infusion or
immersion approaches.

Under this framework, college courses dedicated to critical
thinking would fall in the general category, but integration
of critical-thinking instruction into discipline-specific
coursework could be explicit (infusion), implicit (immersion), or a blend (mixed).

With this framework, Ennis asserts that, since critical
thinking is most often applied to some subject matter, inclusion of critical-thinking content in traditional subjects
(whether through the infusion, immersion, or mixed approaches) is not necessarily inferior to standalone critical-
thinking instruction (the general approach). He also
argues against the notion that critical thinking is so widely
different in different domains of knowledge that only an
immersion approach can manage these differences. As he
points out,

There are many inter-field commonalities in critical thinking, such as agreement that conflict of interest counts against the credibility of a source, and agreement on the importance of the distinction between necessary and sufficient conditions. Fields differ, but ... there is also a common core of basic principles that apply in most fields (though not every principle applies in every field).[23]

Transfer

Questions regarding which approach to take are relevant to one of the key goals of critical-thinking education: *transfer*, that is, the ability of students to take the knowledge and skills learned in one subject and apply them to another subject or to aspects of their lives separate from academics.

When educators argue for the relevance of what they teach beyond the classroom, they make claims regarding the applicability of the knowledge and skills they cover to other domains, a characteristic that provides students with continuing advantages as they move into further, more advanced education or employment.

As educational priorities shifted to STEM (science, technology, engineering, and mathematics) subjects over the last several decades, one argument humanities and social sciences teachers frequently make is that their classrooms provide students with the means to develop transferable critical-thinking abilities. The writing teacher, after all, is not teaching her students to masterfully create a single essay but is training them in writing and thinking skills that can be applied in many situations throughout their lives. Similarly, the ability to discuss and argue positions in a history class based on sound evidence and logical reasoning is a vital skill for decision-making and persuasion well beyond the classroom.

Such transfer claims imply that specific learning activities, such as writing and discussion, teach general critical-thinking skills like logic, argumentation, the weighing of evidence, and persuasive communication explicitly through Ennis's infusion approach or implicitly through immersion. This implication raises two questions, however. First, do teachers trying to develop these transferable skills in students have enough training and experience in teaching elements of critical thinking explicitly as part of an infusion process? Second, are the tools of reasoning so second-nature that immersion in well-taught subject-specific classes will create critical thinkers by osmosis?

These questions also apply to math and science teachers who might claim that their fields provide students the opportunity to hone and practice their critical-thinking ability. For example, one of the first opportunities students have to experience logical arguments occurs when they are taught geometric proofs in math class. Yet how many math teachers take this occasion to show students how premises that provide reasons to believe conclusions can be applied to any form of argument, including arguments that, unlike math, are not based on deductive reasoning? Similarly, how many science teachers stress that the methods they teach can be applied in situations that do not involve the controlled experimentation so bound up in science, such as choosing which college you should attend, or which candidate deserves your vote?

These examples of ways to use instruction on subject-specific content to teach transferable thinking skills gets us to the next question: How should critical thinking be taught?

How to Teach Critical Thinking

The article in which Ennis proposed his four-part framework was subtitled "Clarification and Needed Research." It ended by proposing an ambitious research agenda aimed at determining which of the methods he defines is most effective. In the years since the article's publication, enough research has been performed to inform "meta-analyses" that analyze the results of dozens, if not hundreds, of studies on critical-thinking education practices to identify trends and insights.

One such analysis[24] reviewed the results of 117 "interventions" to improve critical-thinking skills that, in total, involved over twenty thousand primary, secondary, postsecondary, and adult-learner students. The wide range of the age groups, cultures, subjects, and students involved in these interventions makes it difficult to generalize or propose definitive answers regarding what works and what does not. Still, the data from the analysis provide important insights, notably that

> The mixed method, where CT [critical thinking] is taught as an independent track within a specific content course, had the largest [positive] effect, whereas the immersion method where CT is regarded as a by-product of instruction, had the smallest effect. Moderate effects were found for both the general approach, where CT skills are the explicit course objective, and the infusion approach, where CT skills are embedded into the course content and explicitly stated as a course objective.

The researchers also found significant improvement related to teacher preparation, noting that

> When instructors receive special advanced training in preparation for teaching CT skill, or when extensive observations on course administration and instructors' CT teaching practices were reported, the impacts of the interventions were greatest. By

contrast, impacts of CT were smallest when the intention to improve students' CT was only listed among the course objectives and there were no efforts at professional development or elaboration of course design and implementation.

These results jibe with the example described earlier of a successful experiment in the UK in which teachers were given in-depth training on how to implement the Philosophy for Children program. Observations from this large-scale meta-analysis also support the common-sense notions that (1) to learn something, students need to be explicitly taught the subject rather than just be exposed to it and that (2) those teaching a topic must be well-versed in the content (in this case, content related specifically to critical thinking) and specific pedagogies regarding how critical thinking can be taught.

Attempts to create critical thinkers through the schools must also consider the widely held belief, discussed in the last chapter, that critical thinking is not just a body of content to be taught but rather consists of three interconnected components: knowledge, skills, and personal dispositions. This means that becoming a critical thinker involves not just knowing the nuts and bolts of subjects like logic and argumentation but also putting that knowledge to use regularly.

Becoming a critical thinker involves not just knowing the nuts and bolts of subjects like logic and argumentation but also putting that knowledge to use regularly.

Deliberate Practice

In my own work developing curriculum material on critical thinking, which used presidential campaign politics to teach skills like logical reasoning, argumentation, and rhetoric, I was surprised to discover how little time it took to cover the basics of these and many other subjects—for example, media and information literacy and the emotional and reasoning flaws that lead to biased thinking. I experienced something similar while contributing to a program to teach argument-mapping skills to high-schoolers. The time needed to explain mapping took up just a small percentage of the time students needed to learn how to do it. In these cases, and in other instances where critical thinking is taught, the focus needs to be more on skills development through deliberate practice and less on simple instruction.

To understand why, consider the range of diverse and complex real-world situations to which critical thinking can be applied. Understanding how to turn a simple argument in a worksheet exercise into a syllogism or argument map can probably be completed in a few minutes, especially if the exercise is designed to have a correct answer. Arguments "in the wild," however, are rarely defined so simply and clearly. A newspaper editorial, advertisement, or debate performance might contain multiple linked arguments, some strong and some weak, that branch out in all directions. Peering into the logical structure behind these communications or events likely requires substantial translation work to eliminate verbiage and pare the argument down to its essence. Understanding and evaluating the presented arguments might also include further research to discover and then weigh evidence. Such efforts require time, but they give students experience applying the critical-thinking tool set to increasingly complex situations.

How much deliberate practice do you need to become a skilled thinker? Here is one answer, based on the work of K. Anders Ericsson and Neil Charness, from Australian researcher Tim van Gelder:

> Ericsson found that achieving the highest levels of excellence in many different fields was strongly related to the quantity of deliberate practice. Interestingly, Ericsson even found a remarkable uniformity across fields in the amount of practice required to reach the very highest levels; it generally takes about ten years of practice for approximately four hours a day.
>
> Although Ericsson did not study critical thinking specifically, it is reasonable to assume that his conclusions will hold for critical thinking. This means that our students will improve their critical thinking skills most effectively just to the extent that they engage in lots of deliberate practice in critical

thinking. Crucially, this is not just thinking critically about some topic (for example, being "critical" in writing a philosophy essay). It also involves doing special exercises whose main point is to improve critical-thinking skills themselves.[25]

The thousands of hours of practice it may take to become a skilled critical thinker is obviously more than even the most demanding dedicated course on critical thinking can provide, much less a course in a different subject that must balance the development of general and subject-specific thinking skills with the learning of course content. So, perhaps these dedicated and integrated courses need to inform students about the nature and practice of critical thinking and *inspire* them to continue deliberate practice on their own, just as motivated athletes practice for hours each day to train their minds and bodies to anticipate and respond to the ever-changing conditions on the playing field.[26]

Or the combat arena! Few sports, after all, combine deliberate practice over long periods of time with advancement measured through demonstration of mastery than martial arts. This model of skills mastery led Ann J. Cahill and Stephan Bloch-Schulman of Elon University to remake their higher-education class on argumentation along the lines of the martial arts studio:

In such [martial arts] classes, at each successive level of assessment students are also required to demonstrate that they have maintained the skills they achieved in previous belt levels. Importantly, a decent *sensei* does not award a belt on the basis of effort: whether a student has tried hard to master a certain action is not relevant. The question is, can the student throw the punch?

We have applied these insights from martial arts pedagogy to the goal of achieving argumentative fluency, by which we mean developing the ability to understand, evaluate, and construct arguments in such a way that one has the skills, habits and dispositions to utilize these techniques across a broad range of contexts.[27]

The analogy between critical thinking and martial arts training has been drawn out further by Kevin DeLaplante, a former philosophy professor at the University of Iowa. DeLaplante has made it his life's work to teach critical thinking to a wider public through online courses like those offered by his Critical Thinker Academy and a more recent project under development called "Argument Ninja."[28]

DeLaplante's Argument Ninja program would apply martial arts pedagogies to the kind of reasoning skills one might find in a conventional critical-thinking course as well as to insights drawn from psychology about how people interact, especially when they disagree or try to persuade one another. In addition to teaching and providing opportunities for putting critical-thinking skills into practice, deLaplante's is developing a series of belt levels that will give learners the opportunity to meta-cognate on the biases and other psychological factors that obstruct their ability and that of others to reason clearly and objectively.

DeLaplante's goal is to create "rational persuaders," that is, graduates who are capable of using the tools of persuasion to make rational (and, ideally, moral) arguments come across as sound, convincing, and compelling. Such an approach embraces all three parts of the critical-thinking model: acquisition of knowledge, development of skills, and nurturing of personal dispositions related to critical thinking such as curiosity, tenacity, intellectual humility, and intellectual courage. Those dispositions represent intellectual virtues that, like other virtues, are difficult to teach in conventional classrooms but familiar to participants in other learning environments, like the martial arts dojo, sports team, or Scout troop.

Ill-Defined Problems

While research into methods for teaching critical thinking is ongoing, we can draw the following insights from the work already done in this area:

The knowledge related to critical thinking should be taught explicitly, whether as part of a dedicated course or as an integral component of other courses.

Teachers who would like to include critical-thinking content in their courses should be trained on specific critical-thinking skills and how to teach them.

If critical thinking is integrated into another discipline, the integration should provide students with ongoing interaction with critical-thinking techniques rather than relegating critical-thinking topics to one or two classes divorced from the rest of the course schedule.

Students should be given significant opportunities to apply what they have learned through deliberate practice.

Beyond these general principles, there are several innovative educational techniques that can be and have been applied to teaching critical-thinking skills, such as guided discussion and inquiry- and project-based learning. The martial-arts-style argumentation courses described earlier, while novel, also draw from widely used educational methods such as competency-based learning, which bases advancement on the ability to demonstrate mastery of well-defined learning objectives rather than on "seat time" or summative grades.

A common characteristic that differentiates the general use of these techniques from their use in teaching critical thinking is their application in the critical-thinking realm to "ill-defined problems," that is, problems that do not lend themselves to simple solutions or might not have correct and incorrect answers.

Unlike test questions or worksheet exercises with right or wrong answers that can be graded objectively, ill-defined problems are open ended and often involve decisions where there is no obvious solution. These can include problems involving a level of subjectivity or ethical dilemmas that require selecting from options, each with benefits and drawbacks. Such ill-defined problems reflect the complexity of most situations that students need to think about, whether inside or outside the classroom, and are the very situations in learning and life for which critical thinking is required to discover truth or make rational, informed, well-considered decisions.

This notion of ill-defined problems also brings us back to John Dewey's original psychological insights into how people learn. Ill-defined problems engage student curiosity by instilling doubt in their minds, doubt that, according to Dewey's Pragmatic philosophy, we are all highly motivated to eliminate. Given how much of the world does not lend itself to simple, obvious answers, many doubt-generating, ill-defined, open-ended problems are likely to overlap with students' existing interests. The key to successful critical-thinking teaching, then, lies in managing the process students use to resolve doubt, guiding it in intellectually productive ways most likely to lead them to truth or at least to making wise choices.

The ubiquitous presence of ill-defined, open-ended problems provides nearly infinite opportunities for students to explore complex issues on any matter. But the nature of these problems, along with the multipart nature of critical thinking itself, raises another important question related to having development of critical thinkers as an academic goal, especially during an era that prioritizes academic accountability: Can critical-thinking ability be measured?

Can Critical Thinking Be Assessed?

There are a number of commercial critical-thinking assessments used in both academic and employment settings around the world, many of them created by some of the researchers you have read about in this book.

For example, one of the developers of the Watson-Glaser Critical Thinking Appraisal, a popular professionally designed critical-thinking assessment, was Edward Glaser who provided one of the earliest multi-part definitions of critical thinking. Peter Facione, who oversaw the Delphi study to develop agreement on a definition for critical thinking, helped create the California Critical Thinking Skills Test based on the Delphi consensus definition. Given the importance of dispositions revealed through the Delphi Study and other work, Facione and his colleagues also created the California Critical Thinking Dispositions Inventory, a survey-style assessment that purports to measure important intellectual virtues like open-mindedness and inquisitiveness.

Additional published exams, such as the Cornell Critical Thinking Test, the Helpern Critical Thinking Assessment, the Ennis-Weir Critical Thinking Essay Test, and the Collegiate Learning Assessment (CLA and CLA+), have their own focuses and structures, although some research indicates high levels of overlap between what several of these tests claim to measure.[29] Other professionally designed exams, such as the Law School Admissions Test (LSAT) required for applying to US law schools, include logical reasoning questions that are general versus law-specific.

In addition, if we assume that every general critical-thinking course taught at the college level includes quizzes, exams, assignments, and other forms of evaluation, then a wide variety of assessments on critical-thinking skills are being created or implemented at the classroom level. This would also include subject-specific tests and assignments given to students in primary, secondary, and postsecondary school in which higher-order thinking skills are evaluated, such as the ability to write a persuasive essay based on logically valid arguments and well-supported evidence.

This wide range of attempts to measure critical-thinking skills, some of them undertaken by researchers who have spent years studying or teaching the subject, indicates that measurement of critical-thinking ability is possible. But does it work?

Here is where an item in the critical thinker's toolkit, background knowledge, can help us better understand the role assessment can play in determining if someone possesses the knowledge, skills, and dispositions required to be a critical thinker, or how well students are developing those abilities throughout their education.

Professional Test Development

Specific background knowledge I'll be drawing on to help answer questions regarding the nature and effectiveness of critical-thinking assessment comes from the field of professional test design, which uses scientific methods to create standardized academic, professional licensure, and commercial high-stakes examinations.

The professional-test-development process starts not with writing questions but with research and planning focused on determining what needs to be measured. A swimming test, for example, does not just require someone to jump into the water and do whatever they want but rather

This wide range of attempts to measure critical-thinking skills, some of them undertaken by researchers who have spent years studying or teaching the subject, indicates that measurement of critical-thinking ability is possible. But does it work?

measures their ability to perform a specific set of activities such as swimming certain strokes correctly or treading water for a required amount of time. In this case, those activities represent the *construct* that will determine a defined level of swimming ability.

For standardized academic tests, the construct usually involves demonstrating mastery of a body of content, such as the learning objectives incorporated into state, regional, or national subject-area standards. But constructs can also be less direct. For example, college admissions tests like the SAT and ACT used in the United States are based on a construct that says student ability in language and mathematics translates to college success. Despite decades of research used by the makers of those tests to demonstrate support for this correlation, the fact that a growing number of colleges no longer require applicants to take standardized exams can be interpreted as a loss of confidence in their construct.

While lack of complete agreement on the definition of the concept does not stand in the way of critical-thinking education generally (since teachers take different approaches to the same subject in all content areas all the time), the creation of an exam that purports to measure critical-thinking ability must select some definition that will inform the construct for the test.

For example, the Watson-Glaser Critical Thinking Appraisal describes critical thinking as "the ability to look at a situation and clearly understand it from multiple perspectives whilst separating facts from opinions and assumptions."[30] Based on this definition, literature related to the exam describes it as measuring the ability to separate fact from assumptions, make inferences, evaluate arguments, and draw logical conclusions.

As already mentioned, the California Critical Thinking Skills Test was based on the Delphi definition for critical thinking, and reports results in knowledge and skill areas such as analysis, interpretation, inference, evaluation, explanation, deduction, induction, and numeracy (the ability to interpret quantitative information). Other professional exams begin from alternative definition that are detailed enough to inform the planning and test development process.

The planning phase of test design is also research based, usually involving literature review and input from subject-matter experts. The goal of this phase is the creation of some form of exam "blueprint" which specifies which knowledge, skills, and abilities (KSAs) will be covered in a test, as well as other practical considerations, such as how the test will be administered (e.g., on paper or online), test time, and cost. Only after this research and planning phase is complete does test content creation begin.

When building tests, different sorts of test formats are useful for measuring different sorts of KSAs. For example, personal attributes or behavioral characteristics are often measured using survey assessments that are sometimes filled out by the candidate (called a self-survey) and sometimes by an external rater.

Test questions that have correct and incorrect answers are referred to as *closed* or *selected-response items*. Multiple-choice is the most widely used selected-response item type, although variants like matching and true-false questions also fall into this category.

While the scoring of selected-response items is simple and scalable, since the process can be automated, the items themselves can be quite sophisticated. For example, questions can have complex *exhibits* such as text passages or multimedia that require students to synthesize information or perform calculations or other tasks to arrive at a result that can be used to select the right option in a multiple-choice question.

At some point, a construct gets too complicated or multifaceted to be measured by individual test items. These cases call for *performance-based assessments* that ask students to perform a task, the result of which will be evaluated based on various criteria. The most common performance assessment is the written essay, although other work products (called *artifacts*) can serve as the basis for scoring, as can performed activities such as public speaking evaluated by an observer. Certain performance assessments can also be automated, such as tests on software skills based on simulations of software tools and applications.

In general, test complexity and scalability pull in different directions, which is why the most widely used tests, such as standardized academic assessments or college entrance exams, tend to rely on multiple-choice and other selected-response items. This is also why most commercial critical-thinking exams utilize constructed-response items, like multiple-choice questions that evaluate skills such as the ability to make or evaluate inferences or draw conclusions from available evidence. For example, here is a sample test item from Watson Glaser:

> Two hundred students in their early teens voluntarily attend a recent weekend student conference in a Midwestern city. At this conference, the topics of race relations and means of achieving lasting world peace were discussed, since these were the problems the students selected as being the most vital in today's world.

> **Inference 1**
> As a group, the students who attended the conference showed a keener interest in broad social problems than do most other students in their early teens:

True
Probably True
Insufficient Data
Probably False
False

Notice that this test question includes an exhibit in the form of a short reading passages a student must analyze to answer the question. The use of exhibits is common in critical-thinking assessments that ask students to draw conclusions from evidence, with some tests providing multiple exhibits students need to work with to answer a question. This allows selected-response test items to evaluate higher-order thinking skills such as the ability to synthesize information.

Tests that purport to measure dispositions tend to use survey-style questions that ask test takers to rate their level of agreement with statements like these:

"I always do better in jobs where I'm expected to think things out for myself."

"I hold off making decisions until I have thought through my options."

"I try to see the merit in another's opinion, even if I reject it later."

These sorts of survey assessments tend to include large numbers of items, including ones that approach similar attributes from different angles, as well as items designed to detect when test-takers might be less than candid in their self-evaluation.

Performance assessments that ask people to perform open-ended work can elicit evidence of more complex interconnected skills. For example, the Collegiate Learning Assessment (CLA+), one of the most well-known, well-respected performance tests for critical thinking skills, provides test takers with a set of sources they can use to write short essay-style responses. While still constrained, this represents a far more open-ended assignment than answering multiple-choice questions, one that allows students to generate their own arguments rather than analyze and critique arguments created solely to appear in a test.

The final stage of the professional test development process is "validation," which involves research to determine whether a test is accurately evaluating the construct. It is important to remember that tests are not "valid" in and of themselves. Rather, test validation consists of gathering evidence, usually through multiple means, that demonstrates that a test is measuring what it purports to measure. These means can include review of exam content by subject matter experts or comparison of test results against independent measures of the same body of knowledge or set of skills. In addition, validation of high-stakes exams usually includes analysis of test results to determine if an exam adversely discriminates against test takers based on race, gender, or age.

What Works?

Like most standardized tests, commercial critical-thinking assessments have been subject to criticism.

For example, assessments based on self-report surveys are sometimes treated with skepticism,[31] given how easy it is for students to "cheat" by simply misrepresenting their opinions or inflating appraisal of their own abilities, either dishonestly or inadvertently. But such concerns apply to any survey, including ones that underlie a century of important social-science research. In order to mitigate such problems, developers of high-quality survey assessments follow the same process of planning, creating, and vetting test items (in this case, the wording of survey questions), and validation of assessment results that all professionally designed assessments undergo. It should also be noted that survey-style assessments are normally used for research purposes, rather than high-stakes situations like determination of grades.

With regard to tests that use closed-response items, because the exhibits used in many critical-thinking assessments tend to be written, some have raised the question of whether test performance might be a stronger indicator of something other than critical-thinking ability, such as reading comprehension.[32] The use of constrained exhibit material, like arguments meant to be evaluated for certain qualities, also brings up a concern as to whether tests containing only questions of this type let students demonstrate their ability to work with the kind of ill-defined problems most people need to apply critical-thinking skills to real world matters.

Tests for critical thinking also face some of the same challenges presented by tests on general cognitive ability, such as those that purport to measure iQ. These include questions over whether intelligence should be considered an innate, measurable trait, debates over multiple intelligences (including emotional intelligence and creativity) that might not be captured in a test focusing on cognitive ability alone, and whether the whole notion of measurable intelligence is based on cultural assumptions and views of human nature and the human mind that might not be accurate. Even specific test questions, such as the Watson-Glaser example shown earlier, might contain cultural assumptions not applicable across all communities (such as communities where parents of preteens cannot afford to send their children to attend weekend conferences far from home).

These are all reasonable questions which have informed the work of researchers and test developers trying to learn from mistakes of the past, including historic misuse of intelligence measurement applied to both individuals and groups.[33]

Unless one assumes that every commercial critical-thinking assessment and every quiz, test or assignment given in a critical-thinking course is worthless, the real challenge for those who want to measure growth in critical-thinking ability is how to determine which assessments or type of assessments measure the specific critical-thinking elements one is trying to develop in learners. In other words, we are faced not with a lack of tools to evaluate critical-thinking skills, but rather with a wide variety of testing options, each of them based on a different construct of what it means to be a critical thinker.

Critical-Thinking Assessment in the Classroom

The discussion so far has been about professionally designed tests, such as commercially available critical-thinking assessment instruments. Some teachers use published tools, giving such tests at the start and end of a class to determine growth in learning, for example, or as a final exam. It is far more common, however, for teachers to generate their own assessments, designing them to fit the specifics of their curriculum.

The vast majority of testing that goes on in academic environments does not go through the systematic, expensive processes associated with creating valid, professionally designed exams. Rather, academic tests are created by

We are faced not with a lack of tools to evaluate critical-thinking skills, but rather with a wide variety of testing options, each of them based on a different construct of what it means to be a critical thinker.

teachers, who in doing so take on all the roles performed by teams of experts in the professional test-development process: selecting learning objectives to be measured, writing test questions, and grading results themselves or providing guidelines for others, such as teaching assistants, to grade student work consistently.

The advantage of teacher-generated assessments, in addition to their low cost and flexibility, is that teachers can create assessments that exactly mirror the approaches they use to teach the material. They can also explore a range of assessment options that might be too complex or expensive to deliver consistently on a large scale. That said, when students complain that a teacher-written test they have just taken is "bad" or "unfair," they are usually complaining that it has problems such as a lack of content balance, the misalignment of questions with learning objectives, or confusing or poorly designed test items that professional test-development principles, which few classroom teachers have been trained in, are designed to eliminate.

Assessments designed for certain courses can be based on critical-thinking situations and examples relevant to the subject matter being taught. A test of argument analysis skills in a science class, for instance, can look at debates over climate change or human embryo research, while social studies teachers can evaluate those same skills by asking students to locate and evaluate premises and conclusions within historic documents or analyze the logic behind editorials covering current issues.

Without constraints regarding scaling or standardization, teachers can leverage promising assessment technologies such as simulations or "mind-mapping" software that lets students make their thinking visible by mapping out ideas and the links between them. Teachers can also leverage the work of other educators that is increasingly available in online educational communities or use the work of professional test developers to inspire their own assessment designs.

Another evaluation technique particularly relevant for teaching critical thinking is *formative assessment*. These types of assessments are designed not to grade students on what they know and can do (tests that do this are called *summative assessments*) but rather to give a teacher data on individual student understanding so that he or she can provide each student with relevant feedback, ideally in real time.

Simply asking students what they think of the word "argument" at the beginning of a unit on argumentation can serve as a formative assessment if it helps the teacher determine which students associate the term solely with loud disagreements versus those who understand the broader role of arguments in achieving understanding. This knowledge allows the teacher to tailor individual and group instruction and practice activities accordingly.

The exercises needed for the deliberate practice that is so vital to mastering critical thinking—such as ungraded assignments that let students work through problems on their own or with partners—can also be considered formative assessments as long as they are part of a strategy that lets students receive feedback (from the teacher or other students) to refine their work as they learn by doing. In a classroom where formative assessment is doing its job, assessment and instruction should be seamless and, ideally, indistinguishable.

Notice how applying a single critical-thinking principle (background knowledge) provides useful insights into the topic of critical-thinking assessment while also opening up inquiry into other important topics regarding standardized testing and instruction, as well as assessment in the classroom. Given this, let's see what can be learned by using multiple critical-thinking techniques to try to untangle a thorny and complex issue.

Case Study

In the preface, I mentioned *Academically Adrift* by Richard Arum and Josipa Roska, a book that generated tremendous interest and controversy when it was published in 2011. Coverage in many news outlets claimed the book offered proof that students did not achieve any significant gains in their critical-thinking ability during their years in college. Unsurprisingly, such a claim triggered discussion and debate among educators, college administrators, and policymakers.[34]

In some instances, the book's findings fed preexisting narratives of a failing higher-education system, although the discussions it generated about the value of critical thinking were heartening to those of us interested in seeing more resources devoted to helping students develop this vital ability.

Preexisting beliefs and agendas regarding higher education, positive and negative, can be seen as biases that might have distorted interpretations of what the arguments in *Academically Adrift* were and meant. A good critical thinker, however, must control for his or her biases by trying to get to the bottom of what the authors really said and then evaluating the actual argument rather than his or her preferred interpretation of it.

Bracketing out the "noise," we find that the contention of colleges failing to create critical thinkers was based on research that showed students did not achieve gains on the Collegiate Learning Assessment between their first year and their later years in college. This statement of fact allows us to pare Arum and Roska's thesis, which claimed measurable evidence showed student performance in critical thinking did not improve during college, down to this simple, structured argument:

Premise 1: The Collegiate Learning Assessment accurately measures a student's critical-thinking ability.

Premise 2: College students who took the Collegiate Learning Assessment early and later in their college years showed no significant growth in test scores.

Conclusion: College students show no growth in critical-thinking ability during their time in college.

Now one can dismiss this entire argument by claiming that growth in critical thinking is not as vital an outcome for college students as are other goals, such as development of knowledge or exposure to the arts. But assuming you believe in the importance of critical-thinking development in higher education enough to evaluate the above argument, you should recall from the previous discussions on logic and argumentation that this two-premise argument is *valid* because accepting the premises as true requires you to accept the conclusion as true. A valid argument, however must also pass a test of *soundness*. This requires us to scrutinize the premises to determine if any of them are false or at least something a reasonable person might disagree with or doubt.

In theory, the second premise could be false if tests were not scored correctly or if the authors presented their findings in an incorrect or biased fashion. While we should always look for errors or attempts to "cook the books," there is no evidence of this in the careful research presented in *Academically Adrift*, which would make attacking the second premise through speculation uncharitable. It is also unnecessary since a much more vulnerable point of attack is Premise 1.

Given the background knowledge you now have regarding assessing critical-thinking skills, you should understand that a single assessment, even a well-designed, well-respected one like Collegiate Learning Assessment, does not and cannot measure everything that goes into being a critical thinker. The developers of the exam describe the open-ended assessment as measuring "college students' performance in analysis and problem solving, scientific and quantitative reasoning, critical reading and evaluation, and critiquing an argument, in addition to writing mechanics and effectiveness."[35] That is certainly a hefty list of skills, but the conclusion of the argument above is quite broad and definitive, and any general concerns over the ability to test critical-thinking ability, like those you read about in the last section, or questions over the quality and accuracy of Collegiate Learning Assessment itself would demonstrate the argument's lack of soundness and put its conclusion into doubt.

This can be solved by weakening the conclusion somewhat to say that "Students showed no gains in the specific skills measured by Collegiate Learning Assessment during their time in college." In fact, if you read Arum and Roska's original words, rather than relying on the media's interpretation of their results, they seem to reach this more careful conclusion, demonstrating again the importance of background knowledge (in this case, reliance on original source material versus third-party interpretations). The authors also propose mechanisms to explain why students might not be making gains in critical-thinking skills, as well as provide further evidence to support their thesis, such as the aforementioned study identifying a gap between the number of college professors who believe they are teaching their students to be critical thinkers (99%) and the percentage of employers who claim college graduates do not bring critical-thinking skills into the workplace (over 75%).

This additional evidence must come from somewhere. For instance, the gap between professors and employers is based on survey research that can be scrutinized by reviewing the questions on the survey, the number and nature of respondents, and the statistical significance of the results. A critical thinker can continue down this route until he or she has gathered sufficient evidence to determine if the premises forming his or her ultimate version of the argument are true (or at least reasonable) and whether those premises logically lead to the conclusion.

Achieving the Goals of Critical Thinking

Deploying multiple options from the critical thinker's arsenal allows us to get closer to an accurate understanding of what the research behind *Academically Adrift* tells us, which can inform more reasoned and productive discussion than the "sky is falling" debates based on preexisting biases or analyses not informed by logic or background knowledge.

Other hot-button debates, like the ones we have—or fail to have—on important issues like immigration and national security, would similarly benefit from a heavier dose of critical thinking than gets applied in today's media-driven, tribal culture, as would discussions over more everyday matters like whether it's wiser to rent or buy a home, which could improve significantly if informed by the tools of critical thought.

In the last chapter, we will look at what a society that values and prioritizes critical thinking might look like and how we might be able to get there.

WHERE DO WE GO FROM HERE?

In 2011, I visited the Foundation for Critical Thinking's farmhouse headquarters in Northern California, where I had the honor of meeting the organization's founders: Dr. Richard Paul, who sadly passed away a few years later, and its current president, Dr. Linda Elder.

The visit coincided with reports from Japan of the Fukushima nuclear disaster where a nuclear plant, built on a fault line, had failed after being hit by an earthquake and accompanying tsunami, releasing radioactive contaminants into the environment.

"What were they thinking?" we asked ourselves, although in that company we were really considering more specific questions such as these:

What were the premises that decision-makers used to justify placing a reactor in such a vulnerable location?

What logic connected those premises to a conclusion that they should proceed with the project?

As it turned out, the premises were faulty, based on wishful thinking and best-case scenarios. They were also corrupted by regulators beholden to those who wanted to see nuclear power use expanded in Japan. This created biases that affected the decision-makers' choice of what inferences to make and which evidence to believe. Like the plant itself, the argument to place Fukushima where it was placed was formed using unsound building material and a flawed design.

Today's political environment provides another example of what happens to individuals and a society that ignore the principles of critical thinking. No doubt there are voters who give opposing political candidates a fair hearing, taking the entirety of candidates' personalities and political careers into account before passing judgment on them, as well as analyzing where they stand on important issues. Party affiliation (which indicates shared values with other voters) and strong political beliefs (which ranks one's priorities) do not necessarily have to blind us to the possibility that "the other side" is saying something worth listening to. Yet how many of today's voters automatically reject listening to anyone they do not already agree with, or engaging in any form of reflection or deliberation, preferring instead to Google for uncharitable caricatures of

Today's political environment provides another example of what happens to individuals and a society that ignore the principles of critical thinking.

the candidate they never planned to vote for under any circumstances, caricatures constructed from truncated video snippets and out-of-context quotations thoughtfully provided by others?

Many of those "others" are professionals skilled at taking advantage of the flaws in our mental faculties, such as the many cognitive biases that prevent us from thinking critically or the ability of emotion and tribalism to overwhelm reason. Historically, these "others" were the candidates who decided how they would pull the wool over voters' eyes or appealed to emotion or tribalism versus reason. As demonstrated in recent elections, candidates still spearhead this kind of manipulation, but now they are supported by armies of political consultants skilled in techniques for preventing people from thinking clearly.

One would hope that hostile foreign powers using those same techniques to manipulate citizens of other countries—stoking outrage in order to create rifts that put democracy in peril—would wake us to the dangers of abandoning reason for more primal preferences. Yet, has the public appetite for bad premises (i.e., "fake news"), invalid logic, refusal to develop or apply background knowledge, and uncharitable behavior toward our political enemies diminished at all since we learned how vulnerable we make ourselves by basking in our biases? Does our tendency to retreat into bubbles where we only talk to the like-minded or our penchant to shame rather than engage with those who disagree with us make us feel any more empowered? If we continue to reject the intellectual virtues, along with thousands of years of wisdom that can teach us how to be independent and truly free critical thinkers, we should not be surprised if the only people we get to vote for are those who believe they have our number (and probably do).

Catastrophic decisions like those that lead to nuclear plant disasters or being ruled by men and women competent in nothing but playing to our weaknesses are just the most dramatic consequences of refusing to develop or use our reasoning ability, an ability that sets us apart from other animals, which is made infinitely more powerful through techniques available in the critical thinker's tool bag.

We have all made decisions by gut instinct or after "sleeping on it." We have also made decisions after careful research and time spent analyzing our choices. In many cases, the instinctive or spontaneous choices work out well, but compare your personal experiences of decision-making through thoughtful consideration and deliberation versus "winging it." If we can increase our odds of success by locating and evaluating evidence, putting it into an informative structure, and analyzing the results, why not follow this critical-thinking process rather than shooting first, aiming later? Similarly, might testing and, if need be, abandoning a hypothesis about how the world works help us better understand how it actually does?

Turning from personal decisions to interpersonal relationships, if you're like me, you've had arguments with colleagues, friends, or loved ones in which you seem to be arguing past one another. Well, now you know why. More likely than not the argument turned on a hidden premise (one of Aristotle's enthymemes) and, without the ability to find the structure beneath the words, you were left arguing without fully understanding what you were arguing over. Similarly, since you now know the difference between an argument and a fight, you also know how to participate charitably in the former, which is a constructive interaction, and avoid the latter, which is an unproductive and often destructive confrontation.

The good news is that better living through better thinking does not require us to remake the human species. Rather, it simply requires us to use reasoning faculties we already possess a bit better and a bit more frequently than we do now.

With all its successes, science is often held up as a model for systematic reasoning. Yet if you look at science not as a unique activity engaged in only by special people, but rather as a cultural approach designed to slightly diminish the confirmation biases that tend to make all people (including scientists) believe untrue things, you can begin to see the huge payoffs that come from small improvements in how we think.

Another fear that should be dispelled is that becoming critical-thinking individuals in a critical-thinking society would require us to transform Earth into the planet Vulcan. Denizens of that fictional *Star Trek* world claimed to be governed entirely by logic, although it would be more accurate to say Vulcans suppressed the emotions that they believed interfered with logical thinking. With all due respect to Surak, the great lawgiver who founded the Vulcan way of life, such suppression of emotion is a mistake, even for critical thinkers hoping to up the role of logic in their lives.

It is a mistake because emotion, as well as instinct, provides valuable information that can inform the premises of a logical argument. As a parent, many choices I have made (from deciding my kids were ready for bed, or ready to start learning critical thinking) were based not on academic reports and NMR readouts of my children's brain activity, but on the emotional attachment that allowed me to "read" those I loved even before they could utter a word. It is obviously important to interrogate those premises to make sure the emotion informed rather than distorted them and to become more Spock-like when constructing and analyzing an argument that will make use of those premises. But by balancing our emotional, intuitive, and reasoning selves, we avoid cutting ourselves off from valuable data required to apply reasoning effectively in a world made up of people rather than machines.

Even holding strong beliefs and aligning with others who share them, by participating in causes or joining a political party, does not require one to abandon reason for dogma or tribe. In fact, interrogating one's beliefs can strengthen them by helping you determine if they are built on strong foundations of evidence and logic. If they are, you can advocate for them with even more vigor, increasing the possibility of drawing others to your side. If they are not, you can shore them up or even change your mind if you end up realizing your reasons for belief might not be justified. Dedicating this kind of mental activity to the things we hold to be most important to us should be seen as a sign of strength, rather than weakness. Reflecting back on today's political climate, it is not clear that walking away from these critical-thinking principles has made us more empowered, or even happier, human beings.

Presuming you buy the argument that thinking critically more often can improve our lives personally, interpersonally, and politically and that we can become critical thinkers without rebuilding the species, the question that remains is how exactly do we create individuals who think more carefully and in better ways along with a society that appreciates a critical-thinking approach to life's important choices?

Fortunately, those who need to participate in such a transformation are already on board. Most teachers, academic administrators, and educational policymakers

The question that remains is how exactly do we create individuals who think more carefully and in better ways along with a society that appreciates a critical-thinking approach to life's important choices?

believe that teaching critical thinking must be a priority, and employers want to hire more people who possess high-quality reasoning skills. Parents do not want to raise unemployable dummies, and kids have been shown to respond well at all grade levels when critical-thinking topics are included in the curriculum. The wide gap between the high percentage of educators who claim to prioritize critical-thinking education and the low percentage of employers who think graduating students have learned important critical-thinking skills demonstrates substantial room for improvement, but not a lack of motivation or shared goals.

Another bit of good news is that we do not need to spend another two or three decades arguing over definitions of critical thinking in order to accelerate its adoption and practice. To steal an analogy from paleontologist Stephen Jay Gould, "Einstein's theory of gravitation replaced Newton's, but apples did not suspend themselves in mid-air pending the outcome."[1] Similarly, we do not need to await a consensus that will likely never arrive to take advantage of the knowledge and techniques available now, some of them with two-and-a-half thousand years of practice behind them.

In theory, a complete rewrite of the curriculum around higher-order thinking skills could get us where we want to go, but such a major transformation is impractical and improbable given that we no longer live in an era in which some Committee of Ten will come up with a standardized curriculum that everyone will adopt. There are also many legitimate competing priorities in education, such as teaching students to read and write, understand math and science, or become physically fit and socially adept, as well as supporting the many kids with unique needs. These priorities must live alongside the desire to teach students to think well, even if critical-thinking skills can be applied to all these other goals.

If we are to build on what we know, as spelled out in the last chapter's discussion of teaching critical thinking, with an understanding of the constraints under which educators operate, we should put resources into helping teachers learn how to integrate *explicit* critical-thinking instruction and *deliberate practice* into the disciplines they already teach in ways that encourage *transfer*.

You have already read examples of the math teacher using geometric proofs to introduce students to the general principles of deductive argumentation or the science teacher applying the scientific method to more than just science. Such seemingly small changes in methods and priorities could lead to big improvements in general critical-thinking ability, and many teachers have already internalized ways of thinking critically about their disciplines, even if they do not have experience teaching those ways explicitly or tying them to deliberate practice that promotes transferable reasoning ability.

John Dewey's 1910 *How We Think*, "Ground Zero" for understanding and teaching critical thinking, also points to techniques likely to help today's educators accomplish the goal of creating reflective thinkers.

If you recall, Dewey's ideas were based on a Pragmatic notion that students are motivated to think by a desire to dispel doubt, but that doubt is not created in student minds when teachers have all the answers. So, new teacher training, resource-distribution, and pedagogical strategies should emphasize replacing (or at least supplementing) worksheets and tests built from problems with right and wrong answers with questions and puzzles designed to instill motivating doubt, coupled with techniques for guiding thinking in ways that dispel that doubt in intellectually productive ways. Such practices can help students form habits of mind that will persist as they progress from grade to grade and, one hopes, transfer from subject to subject, and from school to life.

Within our lifetimes, most of us have experienced the application of new educational priorities that receive dramatic levels of support at the national, local, and even classroom level. Some of these priorities have grown out of an accountability movement advocating rigorous academic standards and regular testing to determine if students are making adequate progress. Whatever one thinks of these priorities, we have seen governments, educational systems, nonprofits, and the private sector rally to accomplish a common educational goal. If genuine support for critical-thinking education could achieve even a fraction of this support, here are some leverage points to target:

Priorities for Educators

1. Make sure new academic standards embrace transferable critical-thinking principles

As you have already read, important standards like the United States' Common Core emphasize thinking skills associated with activities such as argumentative writing. Similarly, a new generation of science and social studies standards reach beyond knowledge-based content into critical-thinking territory with new categories of standards such as crosscutting concepts that span scientific fields or dimensions focused on developing questions, evaluating sources and using evidence in history and other social studies subjects.[2] If the development of transferable critical-thinking skills is to become a genuine educational priority, rather than just a talking point, skills described in this book should inform ongoing development and implementation of standards across all disciplines at the state and national levels.

2. Modify current systems for preparing teachers to integrate explicit instruction on critical-thinking

principles and deliberate practice of critical-thinking skills into their content-based lessons

Ways of teaching content are covered in methods courses in most schools of education, courses that emphasize general pedagogy as well as techniques for teaching specific subjects, such as math and history. Modifying those courses so that they cover methods for integrating explicit instruction of critical-thinking principles and opportunities to practice critical-thinking skills can accelerate the mainstreaming of infusion and mixed strategies for teaching critical-thinking skills described in the last chapter. Given high turnover in the teaching profession, including large numbers of expected retirements over the next decade, modifying these methods courses to emphasize critical-thinking instruction and practice can accelerate change without disrupting the overall structure of the curriculum.

While seemingly straightforward, such change must contend with challenges facing teacher education generally, best described by Arthur Levine, at the time the president of Teachers College at Columbia University, in a 2006 report titled *Educating Teachers* that criticized university-based teacher education programs "that suffer from low admission and graduation standards" and other failings.[3] These and similar criticisms have led to efforts to improve teacher preparation programs that could create an opening to make preparing teachers to help the next generation of students improve their critical-thinking ability part of wider reform efforts.

3. Investing in professional development for in-service teachers

In-service teachers can learn the same topics and pedagogical techniques described in the last point regarding methods courses though the training they receive as part of ongoing professional development (PD). In many countries, teachers are required to engage in ongoing training to obtain licensure or relicensure, increases in salary, or career advancement. These requirements have created large markets for college courses, in-school workshops, off-site training seminars and online learning options designed to help teachers meet professional-development goals.

While many decisions regarding PD are made locally, educational policy is a major driver of which subjects will be prioritized, best exemplified by the widespread PD that takes place to support teachers when new academic standards are rolled out. If the improvement of students' critical-thinking abilities moves from aspiration to concrete policy, professional development resources are likely to emerge to support these priorities, as they did when accountability became an educational policy driver decades ago.

As with preservice teacher education, the quality and effectiveness of professional development programs have been challenged, with research demonstrating limited impact of PD has on changing teaching practice.[4] Fortunately, new priorities emerging in PD, such as ongoing training (versus "one-and-done" workshops), teachers working together in learning communities, and certification of implementation in the classroom are all reforms that fit well with the learning and practice required to become a critical thinker.

4. Raise the profile of educational institutions and individual teachers already embracing critical-thinking education

Publicizing and celebrating places of learning, including public and independent schools that embrace the 4Cs, as well as organizations outside schools (such as after-school or enrichment programs) that support or experiment with ways of teaching that embrace critical-thinking principles, are other ways to leverage what's already working. Similarly, individual teachers implementing practices that help students develop their critical-thinking ability can serve as inspirations and exemplars for other educators.

5. Provide educators working in the classroom the resources they need to succeed

Teachers are increasingly moving away from textbooks or curriculum packages provided by academic publishers to open educational resources (OER), such as lesson plans, assessments, and learning activities available for free or at minimal cost over the internet. Many of these resources are created by teachers to share with one another[5] or developed by experts working for organizations dedicated to improving education.

Given the wide variety of material available through diverse platforms, locating relevant, quality resources is an ongoing challenge for teachers embracing OER. A commitment to creating high-quality content that supports the teaching of critical thinking that can be easily found online and implemented in the classroom would allow educators to take advantage of proven tools and methodologies that do not require them to recreate what already exists.

These policy recommendations for new priorities imply that school is the best place to create critical thinkers, but by the time students arrive to class they may already be at a deficit, suffering from the crippling biases they receive from home or from peers who embrace beliefs without reflection. This makes home and other environments outside of school the places to teach the intellectual virtues associated with critical-thinking dispositions. Some ideas for doing so include:

Priorities for Families

1. Commit to becoming critical thinkers ourselves

As already mentioned, putting critical-thinking techniques into practice provides individuals of any age with methods for making better decisions, resolving differences, and helping to build a better society. While much of the discussion of education you have read so far deals with teaching younger learners, a wide variety of books, courses, and other resources (many free—including ones listed in the Resources section) are available to help anyone of any age begin a lifelong journey of becoming a critical thinker. Just as it is never too early to start mastering critical-thinking skills, it is also never too late to do so.

2. Practice the intellectual virtues at home

To learn intellectual virtues such as open-mindedness, intellectual humility, and faith in reason, young people need to see them explained and practiced. This means homes where dogmatic politics or hostility to other people's beliefs should be seen for what they are: an unintended brake on children's ultimate success and happiness.

3. Embrace doubt, but channel it productively

If you recall from the discussion of pragmatic philosophy in chapter 2, Charles Peirce's four ways of eliminating doubt include an *a priori* method (continuing to believe what you already believe or what makes you comfortable), *authority* (believing what you are told by authority figures or society), *tenacity* (embracing your own independent beliefs and holding on to them fervently) and scientific reasoning based on hypothesis-formation, experimentation, and refinement of beliefs that create opportunities to get closer to truth. If confirmation bias and tribal thinking that are the causes of so many of today's problems derive from excess reliance on a priori and authority-based ways of thinking, the tendency of adolescents and young adults to rebel against the beliefs of their parents, teachers, and society can be seen as a natural embrace of tenacity that occurs when young people are trying to form their own identities.

Parents with strong beliefs about politics, religion, or other important matters often struggle during this phase of their children's lives. But if we look past such tenacious rebellion to the motivating doubt driving it, there are ways to channel that doubt more productively than insisting our children embrace what we believe or accept their abandonment of important ideas and values, simply because they are held by adults. For example, we can ask them to reflect on and justify ideas they feel passionately about, giving them the opportunity to engage in respectful dialog where changing one another's mind is a genuine possibility. They can also be offered ways of putting their ideas to the test through steps associated with scientific reasoning or through other methods of structured analysis associated with critical thinking. While such reflective activity might end in a stalemate in any one conversation, creating the norm of respectful, reflective dialog demonstrates to everyone involved (children and adults alike) the value of thinking critically about subjects that matter.

Creating a Culture of Critical Thinking

A final thought, more aspiration than prescription, is that societies already rewarding physical strength and prowess on the athletic field, as well as mastery of facts needed to score big on quiz shows, should find some way to culturally celebrate not just what people know but what they can do with that knowledge when thinking critically about a problem or issue.

It has not been that long, after all, since study of subjects like logic and rhetoric defined what it meant to be a thoughtful, educated person—a characterization with a two-thousand-year-history. If we can put scientists on a pedestal for their breakthroughs and contributions to humanity, might we be able to similarly lionize the thinking processes that have led to those breakthroughs while showcasing how scientific and other forms of structured reasoning can help us make smarter choices and believe more true versus false things?

Alternatively, we could treat critical-thinking skills as comparable to "super powers" possessed or developed in a fortunate minority who have the training and willingness to peer through the communication that blankets us to the actual arguments beneath, who can evaluate those arguments for quality as well as use their own skills in reason and persuasion to accomplish their goals (for good or ill). But such an inegalitarian approach ignores the fact that reason is universal among our species, and the ability to reason well is something that benefits all of us since many less-appealing alternatives—such as rule by the mob or demagogues—will always be available to those who eschew a critical-thinking approach to life.

Abductive Reasoning
A form of reasoning that tries to find the simplest and/or most likely explanation for observed phenomena. Also referred to as "inference to the best explanation."

Anchoring Effect
A heuristic or cognitive bias that involves fixing (or "anchoring") a quantity in someone's mind before asking them to examine quantitative information or make a judgment based on numbers or values. For example, the asking price of a house will often become the starting point that anchors the buyer's perception of what a house is actually worth. See also **Cognitive Bias**.

Argument
A set of statements that provides evidence in support of a conclusion.

Argument Mapping
A graphical method for analyzing arguments that involves turning the language of written or spoken arguments into claims, organized so that any claim below another claim provides a reason to believe the claim above.

Bloom's Taxonomy
A hierarchy of learning objectives, published in 1956 and updated in 2001, that organizes learning based on levels of cognitive complexity.

Charity/Principle of Charity
A philosophical rule that asks you to engage with the strongest version of an opponent's argument, as well as to translate other people's arguments into premises and conclusions the originator of the argument would agree reflects the meaning they were trying to convey.

Cognitive Bias
Flaws in mental reasoning resulting from the use of mental shortcuts, called *heuristics* (see **Heuristics**) that can distort judgment, such as confirmation bias that makes it easier to accept evidence and arguments that align with what you already believe.

Committee of 10
A group of educators, led by Harvard president Charles Eliot, that came together in 1892 to establish a standardized curriculum for American schools still largely in use today.

Conclusion
The part of an argument you are asking someone to believe is true if they accept the premises of the argument as true.

Confirmation Bias
See **Cognitive Bias**.

Construct
In test development, the combination of knowledge, skills, abilities, aptitudes, and/or attitudes a test is designed to measure.

Deduction or Deductive Reasoning
A form of reasoning in which accepting the premises of an argument requires you to accept the argument's conclusion. A mathematical or geometric proof is an example of a deductive argument.

Deliberate Practice
Systematic practice of a skill that is designed to provide opportunities to increase ability in the area being practiced.

Dispositions
Personal characteristics that lead to a specific kind of behavior. For example, curiosity is a disposition that can lead people to ask questions and try to discover answers to those questions, making it an important disposition for becoming a critical thinker.

Economy
A principle in argumentation that asks you to make an argument using the fewest number of premises necessary to support the conclusion.

Enthymeme
A hidden premise contained but not stated outright in a spoken or written prose argument.

Exhibit
In test development, a text passage, image, or other type of media that provides information necessary to answer a test question.

Fallacy
A logical flaw that causes an argument to fail. Formal fallacies involve flaws in the structure of an argument, while informal fallacies involve issues related to the language used in the premises and/or conclusion of the argument.

Formal Logic
A form of logic concerned with the way arguments are structured, rather than the language used in the statements making up the argument.

Formative Assessment
A form of assessment (usually ungraded) designed to determine what a student knows or does not know in order to help a teacher provide timely feedback based on an understanding of what the student needs to learn.

Heuristics
Mental techniques or pathways designed to quickly solve a problem or answer a question. In many cases, these shortcuts can lead to systematic flaws in reasoning (see **Cognitive Bias**).

Hypothesis
A proposed answer to a question or solution to a problem that is held as conditional while data is collected and tests performed to determine if enough evidence exists to raise the hypothesis to the level of a theory (see **Theory**).

Inductive Reasoning
A form of reasoning in which accepting the premises of an argument does not require you to accept the argument's conclusion as certain. Inductive arguments are judged as strong and weak, normally based on the probability of a conclusion following from the premises.

Inference to the Best Explanation
See **Abductive Reasoning**.

Informal Logic
A form of logic concerned with how arguments are constructed and the language used in the the the statements making up the argument.

Information Literacy
A method of research, developed in the library science field, for locating, evaluating, organizing, synthesizing, and communicating information, increasingly from online sources.

Logical Form
The abstract structure of an argument, which can be expressed symbolically, separate from the words that make up the argument.

Metacognition
Being aware of and thinking about your own mental processes.

Paradigm
A way of thinking about the world ingrained in an individual, group, or society. For example, Newton's theories created a paradigm for thinking of the universe in terms of mechanical processes that could be explained mathematically.

Premises
Statements in an argument that the arguer is asking you to accept as true and further claiming that those premises lead logically to the argument's conclusion.

Pre-Socratics
A group of early philosophers that preceded the ancient Athenian philosopher Socrates. Their work focused on physical and scientific explanations for natural phenomena.

Rhetoric
Techniques and methods for persuasive communication.

Selected-Response Item
In test development, a question that has a correct or incorrect answer. Multiple-choice is an example of a selected-response item format.

Soundness
In logical argumentation, an argument is sound if (1) it is valid (see **Valid Argument**) and (2) the premises of the argument are true.

Summative Assessment
A form of assessment (usually graded) that determines if students have learned the knowledge or mastered the skills being assessed.

Syllogism
Aristotle's original method for constructing arguments that included two premises (including a major and minor premise) leading to a conclusion.

Theory
A principle that explains a phenomenon. In science, hypotheses (see **Hypothesis**) become theories when they have passed enough tests to be broadly accepted as reasonable within the scientific community.

Transfer
The ability of knowledge or skills to be applied between domains. For example, the successful transfer of scientific reasoning skills might involve being able to apply the scientific method to problems related to history or to personal decisions outside of school.

Valid Argument
A deductive argument (see **Deduction or Deductive Reasoning**) is valid if accepting the premises requires you to accept the conclusion.

Validation
In test development, validation involves amassing evidence that supports the claim that a test measures what it claims to measure.

Warrant
Justification for a belief

NOTES

Preface

1. Barack Obama, "Remarks to the US Hispanic Chamber of Commerce" (speech, Washington, DC, March 10, 2009), The American Presidency Project, https://www.presidency.ucsb.edu/node/286729.

2. From "What Parents Should Know [about the Common Core]," Common Core State Standards Initiative, accessed November 27, 2018, http://www .corestandards.org/what-parents-should-know/. For full information about the Common Core standards, visit www.corestandards.org.

3. US Department of Education, *America 2000: An Education Strategy*, May 1991, 64, https://files.eric.ed.gov/fulltext/ED327985.pdf.

4. Hart Research Associates and the Association of American Colleges and Universities, *It Takes More Than a Major: Employer Priorities for College Learning and Student Success: Overview and Key Findings*, April 10, 2013, https://www .aacu.org/sites/default/files/files/LEAP/2013_EmployerSurvey.pdf.

5. For more information on this OECD research study, which was underway when this book was being written, visit http://www.oecd.org/education/ceri/ Fostering-and-assessing-students-creative-and-critical-thinking-skills-in -higher-education.pdf.

6. Yu Dong, "Critical Thinking Education with Chinese Characteristics," in *The Palgrave Handbook of Critical Thinking in Higher Education*, ed. Martin Davies and Ronald Barnett (New York: Palgrave Macmillan, 2015), 351–368.

7. I turned the *Critical Voter* curriculum into a book published before the 2016 election. Unfortunately, that work seems to have not had great impact on voter behavior. (For information on the project, visit www.criticalvoter.com.)

8. Richard Arum and Josipa Roska, *Academically Adrift: Limited Learning on College Campuses* (Chicago, IL: University of Chicago Press, 2011), 121.

9. Arum and Roska, 35, citing "The American College Teacher: National Norms for 2007–2008," *HERI Research Brief*, March 2009, http://learningout comesassessment.org/documents/brief-pr030508-08faculty.pdf.

Chapter 1

1. *Merriam-Webster's Dictionary*, *s.v.* "chemistry," accessed November 29, 2018, https://www.merriam-webster.com/dictionary/chemistry.

2. Alfred North Whitehead, *Process and Reality* (New York: Free Press, 1979), 39.

3. For a description of how this process unfolded for one important philosophical work, Lucretius's "On the Nature of Things," see Stephen Greenblatt, *The Swerve: How the World Became Modern* (New York: Norton, 2012).

4. In *The Republic*, Plato lays out a metaphysics in which all things in the world, from physical objects to abstractions like truth and beauty, reflect or partake in perfect forms of those objects or abstractions that exist beyond human perception. For instance, any dog we have encountered in our lives is an imperfect worldly example of the ideal form of "dog," just as the true and the beautiful are ideals we can hope to get closer to by studying philosophy.

5. The mechanism whereby one scientific "paradigm" replaces another was described by Thomas Kuhn in his enormously influential 1962 book *The Structure of Scientific Revolutions* (Chicago: University of Chicago Press, 1962).

6. While historians assign different dates to the beginning and end of Europe's Enlightenment Era, for purposes of this discussion it can be thought of as a period that ran through the eighteenth century when ideas generated during the Scientific Revolution inspired thinkers to contemplate how other human endeavors, and society itself, could be reorganized based on human reason.

7. Philosopher Lee McIntyre discusses the culture that instills and supports scientific thinking in his book *The Scientific Attitude* (Cambridge, MA: MIT Press, 2019).

8. Many challenges to claims of scientific knowledge, by scientists such as Pierre Duhem and philosophers like Willard Van Orman Quine, fall into the category of "underdetermination," which highlights that our current evidence might be not be adequate to support explanations of how the world works. While variations in underdetermination are beyond the scope of this book, you can read more about the subject at https://plato.stanford.edu/entries/scientific-underdetermination/.

9. Emily R. Lai, "Critical Thinking: A Literature Review," Pearson Research Report, June 2011, 7, http://images.pearsonassessments.com/images/tmrs/CriticalThinkingReviewFINAL.pdf.

10. See Charles S. Peirce, "The Fixation of Belief," *Popular Science Monthly* 12 (November 1877): 1–15, http://www.peirce.org/writings/p107.html.

11. For example, see Williamson M. Evers, "How Progressive Education Gets It Wrong," Hoover Digest, vol. 4 (1998), available at https://www.hoover.org/research/how-progressive-education-gets-it-wrong.

12. John Dewey, *Democracy and Education* (New York: Free Press, 1997).

13. John Dewey, *John Dewey The Later Works, 1925–1953, Essays and How We Think*, ed. Jo Ann Boydston (Carbondale: Southern Illinois Press, 2008).

14. Dewey, *The Later Works*, 153.

15. Dewey, *The Later Works*.

16. John Dewey, *Experience and Education* (Kappa Delta Pi Lectures, 1938).

17. Dewey, *The Later Works*, 118.

18. Edward M. Glaser, "An Experiment in the Development of Critical Thinking" (Master's thesis, Columbia University, 1941).

19. See chapter 3 for more information on assessing critical-thinking skills.

20. For a summary of the background and process for updating Bloom's taxonomy that includes links to more extensive information on the update, see https://thesecondprinciple.com/teaching-essentials/beyond-bloom-cognitive-taxonomy-revised/.

21. For information on how building on prior learning and other techniques derived from cognitive science can improve teaching and learning, see https://deansforimpact.org/wp-content/uploads/2016/12/The_Science_of_Learning.pdf.

22. Daniel Kahneman, *Thinking Fast and Slow* (New York: Farrar, Straus and Giroux, 2015), 119.

23. Google "invisible gorilla" to see to see an amusing example of flaws in human perception and reasoning.

24. Harry Harmon, Executive Vice Chancellor, The California State University and Colleges, "Chancellor's Executive Order 338," October 29, 1980, https://www.calstate.edu/eo/EO-338.pdf.

25. See Richard W. Paul, "The Critical Thinking Movement: A Historical Perspective," *National Forum* 65, no. 1 (1985), https://www.criticalthinking.org/data/pages/48/4961767a3a4709bf9d4ec478c406391851352ae218fec.pdf.

26. David P. Gardner et al., "A Nation at Risk: The Imperative for Educational Reform," National Commission on Excellence in Education, April 1983, https://www.edreform.com/wp-content/uploads/2013/02/A_Nation_At_Risk_1983.pdf.

27. The reference to an "age of achievement" is taken from Patricia Graham's 2007 history of the American education system, *Schooling America* (see Additional Resources).

28. See, for instance, the OECD research study mentioned in the preface.

29. Hazel W. Hertzberg, "Foundations: The 1892 Committee of Ten," *Social Education* 52, no. 2 (February 1988), https://eric.ed.gov/?id=EJ365372.

Chapter 2

1. For example, a logical argument for the existence of God proposed by Saint Anselm in 1076, called the ontological argument, perplexed many critics who

struggled to explain why it was wrong until the development of modal logic in the twentieth century provided a way to show how the argument suffers from faulty premises. See http://blogs.discovermagazine.com/cosmicvari ance/2011/03/10/modal-logic-and-the-ontological-proof/#.XKHZQJhKg2x.

2. For information on the organization, see https://ailact.wordpress.com/.

3. Internet Encyclopedia of Philosophy, s.v. "Validity and Soundness," https:// www.iep.utm.edu/val-snd/ (accessed March 12, 2019).

4. For more information on how to evaluate informal arguments, including a discussion of ARS (Accuracy, Relevance and Sufficiency) of premises, see the Stanford Encyclopedia of Philosophy; s.v. "Informal Logic," https://plato.stan-ford.edu/entries/logic-informal/ (accessed March, 12, 2019).

5. The Additional Resources section includes books and other material for those interested in exploring further the wide range of logical systems used to perform different types of intellectual work.

6. For a discussion of invalid logical forms, see the fallacies discussed later in this chapter.

7. Inference to best explanation is also referred to as "abduction," a form of reasoning distinct from the deductive and inductive varieties. When scientists attempt to find the simplest explanation for a phenomenon that fits known data (like a heliocentered universe that explains the perceived motions of the sun, moon, *and planets*), they are engaging in abductive reasoning. While preference for simple explanations over complex ones can be seen in early philosophical and scientific ideas (such as Occam's razor, which prefers expla-nations based on the fewest number of assumptions), modern logical systems for abductive reasoning were developed in the late nineteenth and early twen-tieth centuries by the Pragmatic philosopher Charles Sanders Peirce. For more information on abduction, see https://plato.stanford.edu/entries/abduction/.

8. See Nigel Warburton, *Thinking from A to Z* (London: Routledge, 2008). Ex-cerpt at https://nigelwarburton.typepad.com/virtualphilosopher/2007/01/principle_of_ch.html.

9. As with other vast topics intersecting with critical thinking, rhetoric/per-suasive communication is another topic covered by readings and other materi-als in Additional Resources.

10. Richard Andrews, "Critical Thinking and/or Argumentation in Higher Education," in *The Palgrave Handbook of Critical Thinking in Higher Education*, ed. M. Davies and R. Barnett (New York: Macmillan, 2015), 49–62, https:// link.springer.com/chapter/10.1057%2F9781137378057_3.

11. *Merriam-Webster's Dictionary*, *s.v.* "argument," accessed November 6, 2018, https://www.merriam-webster.com/dictionary/argument.

12. *Merriam-Webster's Dictionary*.

13. *Merriam-Webster's Dictionary*.

14. Jay Heinrichs's *Thank You for Arguing: What Aristotle, Lincoln, and Homer Simpson Can Teach Us About the Art of Persuasion* includes a discussion of characteristics distinct to arguments versus fights (see Additional Resources).

15. Matthew McKeon, Internet Encyclopedia of Philosophy, s.v. "Argument," https://www.iep.utm.edu/argument/ (Accessed March 15, 2019).

16. Daniel T. Willingham, "Critical Thinking: Why Is It So Hard to Teach?" *American Educator*, Summer 2007, 8–19.

17. "Information Literacy," University of Idaho Information Literacy Portal, accessed November 25, 2018, http://www.webpages.uidaho.edu/info_literacy/.

18. Originally introduced and used in the fields of engineering and product development, Design Thinking has since spilled into other domains, much of this enthusiasm inspired by the work of the international design firm IDEO.

19. Information on the STEM to STEAM initiatives spearheaded by the Rhode Island School of Design can be found at http://stemtosteam.org/.

20. Dewey, *Later Works*, 115.

21. See www.criticalthinking.org.

22. For a more detailed description of these traits, see http://www.criticalthinking.org/pages/valuable-intellectual-traits/528.

23. This concept derives from Aristotle's work on ethics in which he defined virtue as being the "golden mean" between too much or too little of a trait. For example, the virtue of courage can be found at the appropriate point between cowardice and rashness.

24. Keith Thomas and Beatrice Lock, "Teaching Critical Thinking: An Operational Framework," in *The Palgrave Handbook of Critical Thinking in Higher Education*, ed. M. Davies and R. Barnett (New York: Macmillan, 2015), 93–105, https://link.springer.com/chapter/10.1057%2F9781137378057_6.

Chapter 3

1. "Our Concept and Definition of Critical Thinking," The Foundation for Critical Thinking, accessed November 29, 2018, http://www.criticalthinking.org/pages/our-conception-of-critical-thinking/411.

2. Emily R. Lai, "Critical Thinking: A Literature Review," Pearson Assessments, June 2011, http://images.pearsonassessments.com/images/tmrs/CriticalThinkingReviewFINAL.pdf.

3. Lai citing R. H. Ennis, "A Logical Basis for Measuring Critical Thinking Skills," *Educational Leadership* 43, no. 2 (1985).

4. Lai citing S. Bailin, R. Case, J. R. Coombs, and L. B. Daniels, "Conceptualizing Critical Thinking," *Journal of Curriculum Studies* 31, no. 3 (1999).

5. Lai citing R. J. Sternberg, "Critical Thinking: Its Nature, Measurement, and Improvement," National Institute of Education, http://eric.ed.gov/PDFS/ED272882.pdf.

6. Matthew Ventura, Emily Lai, and Kristen DiCerbo, *Skills for Today: What We Know about Teaching and Assessing Critical Thinking* (London: Pearson, 2017), https://www.pearson.com/content/dam/one-dot-com/one-dot-com/global/Files/efficacy-and-research/skills-for-today/Critical-Thinking-FullReport.pdf.

7. Peter Facione, "Critical Thinking: A Statement of Expert Consensus for Purposes of Educational Assessment and Instruction. Research Findings and Recommendations," report prepared for the American Philosophical Association, 1990, https://files.eric.ed.gov/fulltext/ED315423.pdf, 3.

8. Peter Elbow, *Writing Without Teachers*, 2nd ed. (New York: Oxford University Press, 1998).

9. Peter Elbow, "The Believing Game—Methodological Believing," *Journal for the Assembly for Expanded Perspectives on Learning* 14 (January 2008), https://scholarworks.umass.edu/eng_faculty_pubs/5.

10. Connie Missimer, "Why Two Heads Are Better Than One: Philosophical and Pedagogical Implications of a Social View of Critical Thinking," in *Re-Thinking Reason: New Perspectives in Critical Thinking*, ed. Kerry S. Walters (Albany: State University of New York Press, 1994), 120.

11. Richard Thaler and Cass Sunstein, *Nudge: Improving Decisions about Health, Wealth, and Happiness* (New York: Penguin, 2009).

12. Cass R. Sunstein, *Infotopia: How Many Minds Produce Knowledge* (Oxford: Oxford University Press, 2006).

13. See http://www.battelleforkids.org/networks/p21.

14. Davies and Barnett, *The Palgrave Handbook*, 19.

15. Karen J. Warren, "Critical Thinking and Feminism," in *Re-Thinking Reason*, 155–176.

16. Essays in *The Palgrave Handbook* and *Rethinking Reason* are dedicated to the subject, which can be traced back to Paulo Freire's 1968 *Pedagogy of the Oppressed*, English ed. (New York: Continuum, 1970).

17. Frances E. Jensen and Amy Ellis Nutt, *The Teenage Brain: A Neuroscientists Survival Guide to Raising Adolescents and Young Adults* (New York: Harper, 2015).

18. For details on the P4C trial, see "Philosophy for Children," Education Endowment Foundation, https://educationendowmentfoundation.org.uk/projects-and-evaluation/projects/philosophy-for-children/.

19. For a description of efforts in different countries to include philosophy in the curriculum for learners of all ages, see "Teaching Philosophy in Europe and North America," United Nations Educational, Scientific and Cultural Organization (UNESCO), 2011.

20. Philip Abrami et al., "Instructional Interventions Affecting Critical Thinking Skills and Dispositions: A Stage 1 Meta-Analysis," *Review of Educational Research* 78, no. 4 (December 2008): 1102–1134.

21. For details on the Common Core ELA writing standards for the eleventh and twelfth grades, see "English Language Arts Standards >> Writing >> Grade 11–12," Common Core State Standards Initiative, http://www.corestandards.org/ELA-Literacy/W/11-12/.

22. Robert H. Ennis, "Critical Thinking and Subject Specificity: Clarification and Needed Research," *Educational Researcher* 18, no. 3 (1989).

23. Ennis.

24. Abrami et al., "Instructional Interventions."

25. Tim van Gelder, "Teaching Critical Thinking: Some Lessons from Cognitive Science," *College Teaching* 53, no. 1 (2005): 41–46.

26. While four hours a day is a significant amount of time to dedicate to practicing a skill, the fact that we are thinking during all our waking hours means we have more access to opportunities to practice this skill than do athletes or musicians requiring equipment, instruments or physical locations dedicated to practice.

27. Ann J. Cahill and Stephen Bloch-Schulman, "Argumentation Step-by-Step: Learning Critical Thinking through Deliberate Practice," *Teaching Philosophy* 35, no. 1 (March 2012): 41–42.

28. For more on deLaplante's mission and work, see https://kevindelaplante.com/about/.

29. Jennifer L. Kobrin et al., *Examination of the Constructs Assessed by Published Tests of Critical Thinking*, paper presented at the Annual Meeting of the National Council on Measurement in Education, Washington, DC, April 9–11, 2016, https://www.researchgate.net/publication/301564949_Examining_the_Constructs_Assessed_by_Published_Tests_of_Critical_Thinking.

30. "The Gold Standard Critical Thinking Test, THINK Watson," https://www.thinkwatson.com/assessments/watson-glaser.

31. Kevin Possin, "A Field Guide to Critical-Thinking Assessment," *Teaching Philosophy* 31, no. 3 (September 2008): 201–228. In addition to providing

valuable insights on the use of commercially developed critical-thinking assessments in the classroom, this paper includes an entertaining critique of the self-surveys used to evaluate critical-thinking ability.

32. Kobrin et al., *Examination of the Constructs Assessed by Published Tests of Critical Thinking*.

33. See Scott Barry Kaufman, "Intelligent Testing: The Evolving Landscape of iQ Testing," Psychology Today, October 25, 2009, available at https://www.psychologytoday.com/us/blog/beautiful-minds/200910/intelligent-testing.

34. For details on the controversy surrounding the book, see Kevin Carey, "'Academically Adrift': The News Gets Worse and Worse," Chronicle of Higher Education, February 12, 2012, https://www.chronicle.com/article/Academically-Adrift-The/130743.

35. See "About CLA+," Council for Aid to Education, https://www.cae.org/flagship-assessments-cla-cwra/cla/about-cla/.

Chapter 4

1. Stephen Jay Gould, "Evolution as Fact and Theory," in *Hen's Teeth and Horse's Toes: Further Reflections in Natural History* (New York: W.W. Norton and Co., 1983), 254.

2. See the Next Generation Science Standards at https://www.nextgenscience.org/ and the College, Career and Civic Live (C3) Framework for Social Studies State Standards at https://www.socialstudies.org/c3.

3. Arthur Levine, "Educating School Teachers," The Education Schools Project (2006), available at http://edschools.org/pdf/Educating_Teachers_Exec_Summ.pdf.

4. For details on some of these challenges, see *The Mirage: Confronting the Hard Truth About Our Quest for Teacher Development*, The New Teacher Project (TNTP), August 4, 2015, available at https://tntp.org/assets/documents/TNTP-Mirage_2015.pdf.

5. Teachers Pay Teachers (https://www.teacherspayteachers.com/) is an online marketplace that provides access to several million teacher-developed educational resources for free or at low cost.

ADDITIONAL RESOURCES

Philosophy

Gottlieb, Anthony. *The Dream of Reason: A History of Western Philosophy from the Greeks to the Renaissance*. New York: W.W. Norton & Co., 2016—An accessible, lively study of Western philosophy from the pre-Socratics through the end of the Middle Ages.

Gottlieb, Anthony. *The Dream of Enlightenment: The Rise of Modern Philosophy*. New York: Liveright Publishing Corp., a Division of W. W. Norton & Co., 2017—The second volume of Gottlieb's study of the history of philosophy, which continues through the early modern era.

"History of Philosophy without Any Gaps"—An ambitious podcast series offering a chronological account of the development of Western philosophy, information at https://historyofphilosophy.net/.

"Masters of Greek Thought: Plato, Socrates, and Aristotle"—Audio/video course on the three greatest names in classical Western philosophy, taught by Professor Robert C. Bartlett of Boston College, information at https://www.thegreatcourses.com/courses/masters-of-greek-thought-plato-socrates-and-aristotle.html.

Menand, Louis. *The Metaphysical Club: A Story of Ideas in America*. New York: Farrar, Straus and Giroux, 2007—The Pulitzer Prize-winning study of American intellectual history, including the development of the philosophical school of Pragmatism.

"Partially Examined Life"—This podcast provides listeners with the opportunity to hear a group of philosophers "doing" philosophy through discussion and debate of various philosophical readings and topics, available at https://partiallyexaminedlife.com/.

Wi-Phi Open Access Philosophy—A free resource that features hundreds of instructional videos on various aspects of philosophy, including critical thinking lessons on forms of reasoning, fallacies, and cognitive biases, available at www.wi-phi.com.

History of Science
Alioto, Anthony. *A History of Western Science*. Pearson, 1992—An overview of the history of science from ancient to modern times.

Kuhn, Thomas S. *The Structure of Scientific Revolutions*. Chicago: Chicago University Press, 1962—A groundbreaking analysis of the culture of science which views the field as moving through a series of distinct paradigms that provide different ways of understanding the world.

"Redefining Reality"—Audio/video course that discusses how discoveries in physics, biology and psychology have impacted how we view the universe, taught by Professor Steven Gimbel of Gettysburg College, information at https://www.thegreatcourses.com/courses/philosophy-intellectual-history/redefining-reality-the-intellectual-implications-of-modern-science.html.

Education and Child Development
Graham, Patricia. *Schooling America: How the Public Schools Meet the Nations Changing Needs*. New York: Oxford University Press, 2007—A history of the American public education system traced through a series of discrete stages or "ages."

Jensen, Francis E, and Amy Ellis Nutt. *The Teenage Brain: A Neuroscientist's Survival Guide to Raising Adolescents and Young Adults*. New York: Harper, 2015—A guide to child development through analysis of how the brains of young people grow and change.

"Theories of Human Development"—Audio/video course on the history of theories regarding child development, taught by Professor Malcolm W. Watson of Brandeis University, information at https://www.thegreatcourses.com/courses/theories-of-human-development.html.

Logic and Argumentation
"Argumentation: The Study of Effective Reasoning"—Audio/video course on techniques for logical argumentation and reasoning, taught by Professor David Zarefsky of Northwestern University, information at https://www.thegreatcourses.com/courses/argumentation-the-study-of-effective-reasoning-2nd-edition.html.

E. J. Lemmon, *Beginning Logic*. Cambridge, MA: Hackett Publishing Company, 1978—An accessible introductory textbook covering several systems of logic.

Changingminds.org. "Lists of Fallacies." Accessed November 12, 2018. http://changingminds.org/disciplines/argument/fallacies/fallacies_alpha.htm—An alphabetical list with definitions and examples of over one hundred formal and informal fallacies.

"Think Again"—A four-part course taught by Duke University professors Walter Sinnot-Armstrong and Ram Neta, available from www.coursera.org.

ThinkerAnalytix—Educational resources for teachers and students interested in learning argument mapping, information at https://thinkeranalytix.org.

Rhetoric
Harris, Robert A. *A Handbook of Rhetorical Devices*. January 13, 2013. Accessed November 12, 2018. https://www.virtualsalt.com/rhetoric.htm—Dozens of rhetorical devices explained and illustrated with multiple examples.

Heinrichs, Jay. *Thank You for Arguing: What Aristotle, Lincoln, and Homer Simpson Can Teach Us about the Art of Persuasion*. New York: Three Rivers Press, 2013—An entertaining, practical, modern guide to the art of persuasive communication.

Information Literacy
Information Literacy competency standards developed by the American Library Association (ALA), available at http://www.ala.org/Template.cfm?Section=Home&template=/ContentManagement/ContentDisplay.cfm&ContentID=33553.

Project Information Literacy—A nonprofit organization that provides access to resources and original research on information literacy topics at https://www.projectinfolit.org.

Information on Critical Thinking Assessments Mentioned in Chapter 3
California Critical Thinking Skills Test
https://www.insightassessment.com/Products/Products-Summary/Critical-Thinking-Skills-Tests/California-Critical-Thinking-Skills-Test-CCTST.

California Critical Thinking Dispositions Inventory
https://www.insightassessment.com/Products/Products-Summary/Critical-Thinking-Attributes-Tests/California-Critical-Thinking-Disposition-Inventory-CCTDI.

Collegiate Learning Assessment (CLA and CLA+)
https://cae.org.

Cornell Critical Thinking Test
https://www.criticalthinking.com/cornell-critical-thinking-test-level-z.html.

Ennis-Weir Critical Thinking Essay Test
http://www.academia.edu/1847582/The_Ennis-Weir_Critical_Thinking
_Essay_Test_An_Instrument_for_Teaching_and_Testing.

Helpern Critical Thinking Assessment
https://sites.google.com/site/dianehalperncmc/home/research/halpern
-critical-thinking-assessment.

Watson-Glaser Critical Thinking Appraisal
https://us.talentlens.com/store/ustalentlens/en/Store/Ability/Watson-Glaser
-Critical-Thinking-Appraisal-III/p/100001976.html.

Other General Critical-Thinking Resources
Critical Thinker Academy
Video-based instruction on critical thinking principles by Philosopher Kevin
deLaplante, https://criticalthinkeracademy.com.

Haber, Jonathan. *Critical Voter: Using the Next Election to Make Yourself (and
Your Kids) Smarter*. Lexington, MA: Degree of Freedom, 2016—The author's
book on using election politics to teach critical-thinking skills. Book chapters
and educational resources available at www.criticalvoter.com.

INDEX

infusion method, 123–125, 126, 128

mixed method, 123–125, 128

Teenage Brain, The (Jensen), 117

Tenacity method of belief formation, 20, 179

Test blueprint, 143

Test development process, 140–150

Testing critical thinking skills. *See* Assessing critical thinking skills

Theory, 15

Thinking Fast and Slow (Kahneman), 31

Toulmin diagrams, 63–66

Toulmin, Stephen, 63

Transfer, 125–127, 171

Translating prose into structured arguments, 68–75

 accuracy, 69–71

 charity, 72–75

 economy, 71–72

Tricolon (rhetorical device), 76

Trivium, 6

Tversky, Amos, 29

Twenty-first century skills, xi, 34, 110–113

Undistributed middle (fallacy), 55

University of Chicago, 21, 25

University of Chicago Lab School, 25

Vaisheshika tradition, 2–3

Validation (assessment), 147–148

Validity (logical validity), 40, 71

van Gelder, Tim, 132

Venn diagram, 60–63

Ventura, Matthew, 104

Vulcans, 167

Waldorf schools, 21, 25

Warburton, Nigel, 72

Warrant (Toulmin diagram), 64–66

Warren, Karen J., 115

Watson, Goodwin, 26

Watson-Glaser Critical Thinking Appraisal, 26, 138, 142–143, 145, 149

Watson-Glaser Critical Thinking Test. *See* Watson-Glaser Critical Thinking Appraisal

Whitehead, Alfred North, 3

Willingham, Daniel T., 83

Wundt, Wilhelm, 17

The MIT Press Essential Knowledge Series

JONATHAN HABER is an educational researcher, writer, and entrepreneur working in the fields of critical-thinking education, assessment, and technology-enabled learning whose work has been featured in the *New York Times*, the *Boston Globe*, the *Chronicle of Higher Education*, the *Wall Street Journal*, and other major media sources. He is the author of another MIT Press Essential Knowledge book, *MOOCS*, as well as *Critical Voter: Using the Next Election to Make Yourself (and Your Kids) Smarter,* and coauthor of *National Educational Technology Standards for Students (NETS*S): Resources for Assessment*, published by the International Society for Technology in Education (ISTE).